Definitive Guidance

The Church's Statements on Homosexuality

With a Foreword by Clifton Kirkpatrick
and a Study Guide by Jack L. Stotts

Book design by Teri Vinson
Cover design by Night & Day Design

First edition
Published by Westminster John Knox Press
Louisville, Kentucky

This book is printed on acid-free paper that meets the American National Standards Institute Z39.48 standard. ♾

PRINTED IN THE UNITED STATES OF AMERICA

04 05 06 07 08 09 10 11 12 13 — 10 9 8 7 6 5 4 3 2 1

Library of Congress Cataloging-in-Publication Data

Presbyterian Church (U.S.A.)
    Definitive guidance : the church's statements on homosexuality / with a foreword by Clifton Kirkpatrick ; and a study guide by Jack L. Stotts.—1st ed.
        p. cm.
    ISBN 0-664-50259-8 (alk. paper)
    1. Homosexuality—Religious aspects—Presbyterian Church (U.S.A.)—Textbooks.
    2. Presbyterian Church (U.S.A.)—Doctrines—Textbooks. I. Presbyterian Church (U.S.A.). General Assembly. II. Title.

BX8969.5.p74 2004
261.8'35766'088285137—dc22   2004041164

Contents

Note from the Publisher

Included in this study book are papers from the United Presbyterian Church in the USA (UPCUSA) and the Presbyterian Church in the United States (PCUS) as they were printed in the Minutes of the General Assembly and published by the Office of the General Assembly. The documents are reprinted in their entirety with the following exceptions:

- The study guide that accompanied the 1977 PCUS document, *The Church and Homosexuality: A Preliminary Study,* is not reprinted here.

- For the 1978 UPCUSA document, *The Church and Homosexuality,* the lengthy background paper, which does not have official policy status, has not been reprinted here for reasons of space. It can be found on the Presbyterian Church (U.S.A.) Web site, http://www.pcusa.org/oga/publications/church-and-homosexuality.pdf.

Foreword

Clifton Kirkpatrick, Stated Clerk,
Presbyterian Church (U.S.A.)

The Presbyterian Publishing Corporation has done the whole church a great service by reprinting, with a helpful study guide, the policy statements regarding homosexuality from both of our predecessor denominations, the Presbyterian Church in the United States and the United Presbyterian Church U.S.A. I hope that Presbyterians will use these materials afresh as we continue to discern God's will about issues of human sexuality and ordination, which are as much matters of deep concern for our church and for people throughout our nation today as they were in the late seventies.

These statements are twenty-five years old, but they are remarkably contemporary. In the intervening twenty-five years, the Presbyterian Church has held countless debates and taken a wide variety of actions (Constitutional amendments, authoritative interpretations, judicial actions, and pastoral interventions), but the basic policy of the church has remained constant. That policy is articulated in these documents along with a sociological and theological analysis, study questions, and pastoral suggestions for Presbyterians.

Three basic themes have been the consistent policy of the church over the last quarter of a century:

1. That God created and loves all people regardless of sexual orientation or practice and, therefore, that people of all sexual orientations or practice should be joyfully welcomed as members of the Presbyterian Church (U.S.A.);

2. That the Presbyterian Church (U.S.A.) as a part of its commitment to be an agent of God's justice is called to work

actively against homophobia, against discrimination of gay and lesbian people in church and society, and for full human and civil rights for all people, regardless of sexual orientation; and

3. That God's intention for human sexuality is for it to find ultimate expression only in marriage between a man and a woman, and therefore, self-affirming, practicing homosexual persons are not to be invited to be church officers.

While much debate has occurred and many attempts have been made to amend the church's stance, these policies have basically been sustained over the past twenty-five years. However, especially for the third of these propositions, there continues to be both debate and much pain and anguish in the church. In 2000 the General Assembly created a Theological Task Force on the Peace, Unity and Purity of the Church to, among other things, seek to help the church discern God's will in relation to this and other areas of conflict in the church. As this group invites the wider church to study these matters, this booklet with these historic policy statements and the study guide will be especially helpful. I hope you will make good use of this valuable resource.

This publication also reminds us of the first two, less controversial, basic positions of our church regarding homosexuality: that all of our churches should actively welcome into the membership of the church homosexual persons who seek to follow Jesus Christ and that we should work actively for full human rights of all persons, regardless of sexual orientation. The study of these materials can be a valuable resource to congregations and governing bodies as they seek to make these convictions come alive in their life and ministry.

I wish you well as you use this valuable resource to seek to understand the teaching of our church, to discern God's will for us, and to be faithful in our ministry to all of God's people.

THE CHURCH AND HOMOSEXUALITY: A PRELIMINARY STUDY, 1977

Office of the Stated Clerk,
The Presbyterian Church
in the United States

Actions of the 117th General Assembly Relating To Homosexuality

**From the report of the Standing Committee
on Justice and Human Development**

A. That the paper, *The Church and Homosexuality: A Preliminary Study,* be endorsed as a basis of study.

B. That the 117th General Assembly authorize the distribution of *The Church and Homosexuality: A Preliminary Study.*

C. That the Stated Clerk of the General Assembly be instructed to print the paper, along with a study guide to be commissioned in consultation with the Council on Theology and Culture, and send to all PCUS ministers and Clerks of Sessions. Sufficient copies of the paper should be made available at adequate charge to recover cost of printing and mailing in order to honor additional requests from interested persons.

D. That presbyteries, sessions, individual churches and church members be requested to study the paper and respond with data and suggestions to the Council by May 1, 1978.

E. That a task force appointed, directed and funded by the Council receive the data and suggestions from the Church, continue the study of homosexuality and make further recommendations to a subsequent General Assembly in light of responses received from the Church.

F. In addition, the following statements were adopted:

"That the 117th General Assembly express love and pastoral concern for homosexual persons and the need for the Church to stand for just treatment of homosexual persons in our society in regard to their civil liberties, equal rights, and protection under the law from social and economic discrimination which is due all citizens."

"Although we confess our need for more light and pray for spiritual guidance for the Church on this matter, we now believe that homosexuality falls short of God's plan for sexual relationships and urge the Church to seek the best ways for witnessing to God's moral standards and for ministering to homosexual persons concerning the love of God in Jesus Christ."

—*Stated Clerk*

The Church and Homosexuality: A Preliminary Study

"In studying the following paper it should be remembered that the General Assembly may issue a statement (or pronouncement) for any one or more of the following purposes: to express its own judgment on an issue; . . . to influence the conscience of the Church; . . . to recommend particular actions by individual members, congregations and lower courts; . . . to identify priorities for the denomination; . . . to establish goals for the General Assembly's own agentry; . . . to direct, request, or authorize its own agentry or staff to take certain actions; . . . to commend, petition, or express concerns to the government, . . . (and) to help shape public opinion.

In light of this, it is evident that the General Assembly addresses itself to 'a wide variety of audiences.' However, it must be remembered, that while the General Assembly may speak to these issues and audiences, 'it . . . speaks (only) for itself'. '(It) does not . . . speak for God . . . for all individual members of the PCUS, (nor even does it) necessarily speak for the majority of Presbyterians', . . . and must meet specific constitutional requirements in order to 'speak for the denomination as a whole.' . . . A General Assembly statement is just that—a paper or statement by a particular assembly. These statements or papers may take the form of 'declarations of conscience, . . . moral appeals . . . (or) policy or program

> directives.' As such they should be considered in light of the form in which they are sent and for the purpose to which they have been directed. 'Declarations of conscience have authority . . . only to the degree—that they conform to the Word of God . . . Moral appeals possess only such authority as those to whom they are addressed recognize.' Policy and program directions pertain to the agency created to perform that function.
>
> It is hoped that you will study the following paper, bearing in mind both the importance and boundary of a General Assembly paper or statement." (PCUS *General Assembly* Minutes, *1974, p. 176)*

The 112th General Assembly of the Presbyterian Church in the United States referred to the Council on Church and Society the attached resolution which the 113th General Assembly referred to the Council on Theology and Culture (Appendix A).

The 116th General Assembly referred to the Council on Theology and Culture the following overture from the Presbytery of Fayetteville (attached, Appendix B).

The paper which follows, with its recommendations, is the response of the Council on Theology and Culture to these referrals.

> If we are to think responsibly about homosexuality today, we must learn what the science of human behavior can teach us about its causes and character. We must engage in careful biblical and theological reflection. In our time, when many homosexual persons, some of them committed Christians, are speaking out for themselves, we must listen with compassion and openness to what they have to tell us. The task is not easy. The scientific data are incomplete and inconclusive; psychiatrists, psychologists and sociologists interpret them in different ways. Biblical scholars and theologians committed to the authority of Scripture disagree in their interpretations of Scripture. Homosexual persons themselves do not speak with one voice. There is great variety in their experience, and they are as subject as anyone else to error in the interpretation of their experiences and in their understanding of themselves. Moreover, all of us have trouble thinking clearly about homosexuality because we approach it with various degrees of fear, anxiety, guilt and prejudice based on culturally stereotyped views of masculinity and feminity [*sic*] and sexuality in general. All these complications and difficulties mean that even when we have done the best we can to achieve a faithful and intelligent Christian understanding of homosexuality and homosexual persons, we must be modest about our conclusions and open to let ourselves be corrected as we are led to deeper understanding in the future.

Since the referrals to the Council on Theology and Culture deal with the question of the Church's attitude toward homosexuality, this paper does not deal with the problem of the civil rights of homosexual persons (but see VI. 3h below). The selected bibliography at the end of this study is representative of the various scientific and biblical-theological points of view discussed here.

I. The Definition of Homosexuality

Homosexual means literally "the same sex." In its most general sense it refers to all activities and associations between persons of the same gender. Thus any all-male or all-female club, church group, school, military organization, athletic team, business or recreational association is "homosexual" in this broad sense. In popular usage the word is restricted to explicitly sexual attraction and/or activity between members of the same sex, and it is in this sense that we shall use it. But reflection on the significance of any sexually segregated activity or group could be instructive for people who consider themselves heterosexual, and especially for those who believe that God created male and female for each other.

Even in a specifically sexual context homosexuality is not easy to define. The following considerations show what a very complex phenomenon it is:

1. Homosexuality involves both motivational and behavioral factors. A homosexual person is not only one who engages in physical sexual acts but one with homosexual feelings, wishes, fantasies and desires; not only one whose homosexuality is expressed in doing but one whose homosexuality is expressed in seeing, hearing, thinking and dreaming. Not every homosexually oriented person engages in overt homosexual activity. The absence of overt homosexual activity does not necessarily mean that a person is not homosexually oriented. In defining homosexuality it is thus important to distinguish between but not separate a homosexual "orientation" or "condition" and homosexual activity.

2. Isolated or occasional homosexual experiences at certain periods of life or in unusual circumstances do not necessarily mean that a person is fundamentally homosexual.

3. There is as much variety in the expression of homosexuality as in the expression of heterosexuality: Homosexual persons, like heterosexual persons, may be promiscuous or not, concerned only for physical self-gratification or concerned for loving personal relationships. Homosexual persons may or may not display the physical or behavioral characteristics popularly identified as homosexual ("feminine" men or "masculine" women). Pedophilia (sexual attraction to children) is no more characteristic of homosexual persons in general than of heterosexual persons in general. Some psychiatrists believe that homosexual persons in general are no more lonely, anxious, depressed, lacking in self-acceptance, unproductive, irresponsible in personal and social relations and generally unhappy than are heterosexual persons. In short homosexual persons are as different from each other as are heterosexual persons.

4. Homosexuality may be unconscious as well as conscious. It may be repressed below the level of awareness and then unknowingly expressed in various apparently

non-sexual ways. An exaggerated hatred or fear or repulsion in relation to homo-sexual persons may sometimes be a symptom of such repressed homosexuality.

5. There are degrees of homosexuality. Relatively few people are exclusively either homosexual or heterosexual. Most people fit into a continuum between the two, with varying degrees of both in their psychosexual make-up. Most of us are thus to some extent both homo- and heterosexual. This continuum is an impor-tant factor in answering the question whether a homosexual person's sexual ori-entation can be changed: possibility of change becomes increasingly more difficult the further he or she is from an exclusively heterosexual orientation and the closer he or she approaches an exclusively homosexual orientation.

All these considerations should lead us to be very careful about making simplis-tic statements about homosexuality, about who is and who is not homosexual, and about the character of homosexual persons in general.

II. The Causes and Character of Homosexuality

There are various theories about the causes of homosexuality. Some authorities believe that it is the result of hormonal or genetic or other biological factors. Oth-ers believe that people become homosexual because of distorted relationships early in childhood with either one or both parents. Some sociologists believe that cultural prejudices about what is masculine and feminine may result in the rejec-tion and alienation of a person who does not "fit in" or "measure up" and lead him or her to find acceptance and self-worth in homosexual relationships. Like heterosexual patterns of sexuality, homosexual patterns vary, and both can prob-ably be accounted for only by a combination of psychological, medical and socio-logical factors.

As behavioral scientists do not agree on what causes homosexuality, so they disagree in their evaluations of it.

Some believe that it is a sickness or perversion or emotional disorder and that the attempt should be made to "cure" homosexual persons (though there is disagreement about the possibility of curing those with an exclusive or near-exclusive homosexual orientation).

Other authorities believe that homosexuality is not so much a disease as an arrest in psychosexual development which prevents an individual from growing into the capacity for mature heterosexual relationships. What the homosexual person needs is not so much to be cured as to be "unblocked" so that the normal process of psychosexual development can continue (although there is disagree-ment here too about the possibility of overcoming the crippling effects of past experiences in the lives of some homosexual persons).

Still other authorities take a more neutral position: homosexuality is simply a variation in sexual orientation. They grant that some homosexual persons may be emotionally disturbed but do not believe that the reason is that they are homosexual. If homosexual persons have unique problems, the reason lies in social, economic and religious prejudice and discrimination against those whose way of life is different from that of the majority. Homosexual persons may need to learn to adjust to the difficulties of being a minority, but what needs changing is not homosexual persons themselves but society's attitude toward them.

Finally, some behavioral scientists take an openly affirmative position: homosexual persons should claim, honor and responsibly live out their homosexuality. It is just as natural for them as heterosexuality is for others. For them it would be sick or abnormal to deny or repress their homosexuality.

Whether they tend to be negative, neutral or positive in their attitudes, most researchers qualify their evaluations by acknowledging the limitation of their research and the data it has produced, and by emphasizing the fact that one cannot make broad generalizations which ignore the great variety in the experiences and lifestyle of homosexual persons.

III. Some Fundamental Ethical and Theological Presuppositions

Scientific research into the causes and character of homosexuality cannot answer for us the theological and ethical questions we must ask on this issue. Christians are called not to be conformed to the world and its wisdom but to be transformed by the renewal of their minds through the will of God in Jesus Christ. As we cannot let our moral decisions on other issues be determined by the society and culture in which we live, so we cannot make our decisions about sexuality in general or homosexuality in particular on such a basis. What seems "natural" and "normal" and "right" to behavioral scientists and/or the great majority of people may need to be rejected by Christians. And what seems "unnatural" and "abnormal" and "wrong" to behavioral scientists and/or the great majority of people may need to be affirmed by Christians. Nevertheless the behavioral sciences can help us to be more realistic and responsible in our theological and ethical reflection and decisions. It is especially important to remember the following points:

1. *The individuality of homosexual persons.* The complexity and variety of homosexuality means that it is as wrong to say what "all" homosexual persons are like as to say what "all" black or white, rich or poor, male or female people are like. We can deal responsibly with homosexual persons as with all other persons only when we rid ourselves of stereotyped presuppositions about them and treat each one as the unique human being and child of God he or she is, with his

or her unique problems and needs, limitations and possibilities, strengths and weaknesses.

2. *The Church's involvement.* Scientific research into the causes and nature of homosexuality raises questions not only about homosexual persons themselves but also about those individual persons (parents, teachers and others) and the common cultural values and attitudes which helped shape their sexual orientation. It therefore leads us to ask also what the Church in particular has done or not done to influence those persons and our society. When moral judgments are made in this sphere, they are inevitably moral judgments on ourselves also. The question cannot only be "Why are they like that?" It must also be "What have we the Church done or left undone that has contributed to what they are?" In this sphere as in others we will be more just and more compassionate if we remember the warning of our Lord that we ourselves will be judged with the judgment we pronounce.

3. *The relation between homosexual orientation and homosexual activity.* The distinction and connection behavioral research makes between a homosexual orientation and homosexual activity warns us of the theological and ethical inadequacy of any judgment about homosexualitywhich ignores either.

On the one hand, any judgment based only on homosexual acts would be not only psychologically but also theologically superficial. Christians believe in a God who judges all men and women not just on the basis of external deeds but on the basis of what is hidden (sometimes even from themselves) in the secret depths of their hearts. Any responsible judgment about homosexuality has to be a judgment not only about homosexual activity but also about homosexual feelings, thoughts and desires, whether or not they are acted out. (Although we are concerned here especially with people who are more or less consistently homosexual, this is true of course also with regard to those for whom such urges are more or less occasional and fleeting.)

On the other hand, we must distinguish between homosexual orientation and homosexual activity. While it is true that God judges all people on the basis of what he sees in their hearts, it is also true that it is dangerous for us who are not God and cannot see into the hearts of any other person to make judgments about him or her on any other basis than what he or she does. Moreover, while it is to a greater or less [sic] extent true that none of us can help what we feel or the thoughts that enter into our heads, it is also true that all of us can make decisions about what we will do with those feelings and thoughts. Like heterosexual persons, homosexual persons are responsible for their actions and how they affect others as well as themselves.

A responsible Christian position must thus avoid both a legalistic (and perhaps self-righteous) concentration on explicit homosexual activity and an over-emphasis on homosexual orientation. It must include those who are homosexual "in their hearts" but it must also realistically distinguish between feelings, thoughts and desires on the one hand and actions on the other.

4. *The possibility of change.* We have seen that homosexual persons (like heterosexual persons) are responsible for what they *do*. Are they also accountable for what they *are*—for their homosexual orientation? One way to get at this question is to ask whether they can change their psychosexual condition.

The behavioral sciences teach us that most homosexual people do not simply "decide" to be homosexually oriented, nor can they simply "decide" to stop being homosexually oriented. The psychosexual orientation of many if not all homosexual persons is shaped by influences they did not choose and over which they had little or no control. And the possibility of their changing their psychosexual orientation appears to be increasingly remote the closer they come to an exclusively homosexual orientation.

When we reflect on these clinical and sociological conclusions as Christians, we must avoid the error of the simplistic assumption that homosexual persons can change their psychosexual orientation if they just "want to" or "try hard" (the error of indeterminism). But we must also avoid the error of the resigned assumption that homosexual persons are so completely shaped by external influences that any real change is impossible (the error of determinism). Against indeterminism not only the behavioral sciences but also Scripture teaches us that people can be so dominated by the external influences that shape their lives that they cannot do what they will and cannot help doing what they do not want to do (Rom. 7.18ff). Yet we cannot surrender to psychological or sociological determinism. The behavioral sciences have not proved and Christian presuppositions about human nature do not allow us to accept the claim that human beings are totally the victims of external influences and totally unable to take responsibility for the kind of persons they are and can become. Moreover, Christians who know about the power of God's grace know that what with human beings is (or seems to be) impossible is possible with God. If he so will, God can enable any person to become what that person cannot become by his or her own efforts.

A responsible Christian position on homosexuality must therefore find a way between determinism and indeterminism. To believe that homosexual persons can simply "give up" their homosexuality and "decide" to become heterosexual is both unrealistic and lacking in compassion. But on the other hand, to believe that the homosexual orientation is an inexorable fate imposed on some people is faithless and equally lacking in compassion.

We have now reached the point where general theological and ethical reflection on what we can learn from the behavioral sciences can carry us no further. They can help us recognize the complexity of homosexuality. They can help us avoid simplistic answers which are theologically as well as psychologically superficial. They can suggest some criteria for formulating a responsible Christian position. But, as we acknowledged at the beginning of this section, they cannot answer for us the most crucial theological and ethical questions: What *is* responsible ethical behavior for homosexual persons? *Should* they change—or at least try to change—their psychosexual orientation? What should be the Church's attitude toward them? For help in answering these questions we must turn to the Bible.

IV. Interpretations of Biblical Teaching about Homosexuality

Scripture does not give us as much help as we would like to have with this issue. The biblical texts which are most relevant are Genesis 19.1–11 (perhaps), Leviticus 18.22 and 20.13, Romans 1.18–27, I Corinthians 6.9–11 and I Timothy 1.8–11. In none of these texts is homosexuality the major topic; biblical writers mention it only in the context of discussions of broader themes, suggesting that they have little interest in homosexuality for its own sake. All these passages (with the possible exception of the first) refer to homosexual acts only; none of them deal with the questions raised by what we have learned in our time about the complex relationship between homosexual acts and a homosexual orientation. Nevertheless, within the limited scope of their interest in and understanding of homosexuality, all these passages agree in condemning it.

On the basis of these texts, supported by an interpretation of the biblical understanding of sexuality in general, the whole Hebraic-Christian tradition has consistently rejected homosexuality as unnatural and sinful. In our time, however, this traditional position has been challenged. Some interpreters suggest that a different understanding of homosexuality results from an examination of the relevant texts in light of the time and place in which they were written, in light of a fresh look at the biblical understanding of God's intention for human relatedness in general, and in light of the new insights of the behavioral sciences into the complex causes and nature of homosexuality.

In this section we will summarize this contemporary debate as fairly as possible without attempting to defend or refute any position. The biblical discussion will then form the basis for a discussion in the next section of the alternatives before the Church today as we seek to deal with homosexuality and homosexual persons as faithful and responsible Christians.

A. Old Testament

Genesis 19.1–11 tells the story of the men of Sodom who came to Lot demanding that he let them "know" the two visitors in his home. "Know" here has been traditionally interpreted to mean to know sexually and thus to imply a demand for homosexual acts (thus our word "sodomy"). Sometimes the word unmistakably means this in the Old Testament; more often it does not. Some biblical scholars (including Calvin in his commentary on Gen. 19.5) deny that it has this connotation here. They interpret the story to mean that Lot exceeded his rights as an alien in the city (v. 9) when he entertained two unknown men without presenting them to the permanent residents. The men of the city then came demanding literally only that Lot introduce these strangers to them. (This is also Calvin's interpretation, though he combines it with the traditional interpretation, arguing that the men of the city were really using this legitimate demand as an excuse to capture the visitors for homosexual purposes.) Other Old Testament passages which mention the destruction of Sodom (such as Is. 13.19, Jer. 49.18, 50.40) do not identify the practice of homosexual acts as the sin for which it was destroyed. Ezekiel 16.49f. mentions that the people of Sodom did "abominable things." Some interpret this as a reference to homosexuality, but others point out that in other Old Testament passages it is a common description of idolatry. In any case, this passage mentions specifically another reason for Sodom's destruction: "Behold, this was the guilt of your sister Sodom: she and her daughters had pride, surfeit of food and prosperous ease, but did not aid the poor and needy." In short, the weight of Jewish and Christian tradition (cf. Jude 6–7) is on the side of interpreting the Sodom story as a condemnation of homosexuality; but it has also been argued that the story does not deal with this issue at all.

No such uncertainty exists when we come to Leviticus 18.22 and 20.13. These passages explicitly condemn male (but not female) homosexual acts, the second prescribing the death penalty as punishment. These texts are part of the Levitical Holiness Code which lay down rules for maintaining the ritual, moral and religious purity of ancient Israel and its separation from its pagan neighbors. Homosexual activity is not singled out as an especially terrible sin but along with other practices it is specifically condemned. These texts express the consistent position of ancient Israel.

Some contemporary interpreters question the relevance of these texts for us today, using arguments such as the following: (1) The Holiness Code contains ceremonial and judicial laws which Christians believe may have been important in that time and situation but which are no longer binding on us—laws for instance which forbid the eating of meat with blood in it (Lev. 17.14) and laws which require the death penalty for those who curse their parents (Lev. 20.19) and for mediums and wizards (Lev. 20.27). Is it not arbitrary to isolate the law forbidding homosexual activity as permanently binding and to dismiss other laws as no longer authoritative? If other parts of this ancient code are outdated, why not this particular [sic] also? Does not such arbitrary selection indicate simply the use of Scripture to confirm prejudices we bring to it? (2) Those who emphasize the Levitical condemnation of homosexual acts do not take it seriously themselves.

Few today would insist that the death penalty should be prescribed for such acts. Is it not inconsistent to insist on the divine authority of the prohibition but to ignore the penalty imposed by God? Does not such inconsistency also indicate that the real motivation of those who emphasize these texts is not so much concern for the authority of Scripture as their use of Scripture to confirm their prejudice against homosexual persons? (3) When we ask why homosexual practices are condemned in the Holiness Code, we see the irrelevance of this prohibition today. In ancient times homosexual activity was practiced in connection with temple prostitution and thus with idolatry. Perhaps ancient Israel was also opposed to homosexuality because it prevented the fulfillment of the covenant promises of God to increase the numbers and political power of the people. But no one today connects homosexuality with religious sex rites, and Christians understand that the covenant relationship with God is not connected with procreation. God's people today as in ancient Israel still need to be set apart from their pagan environment and there are certainly some expressions of homosexuality which should be condemned, but when we understand the Holiness Code in its historical context, it gives us no reason to condemn homosexuality as such. (4) Christians base their understanding of the laws given in the Old Testament on what Christ has done both to free us from the law and at the same time to fulfill its intentions in a new way. A Christian position on homosexuality cannot be based on a legalistic use of the Old Testament. This last argument leads us to consider how those who question the contemporary relevance of Leviticus 18.22 and 20.30 interpret the New Testament.

Other interpreters believe that these passages cannot be so easily dismissed: (1) It is true that some of the ceremonial and judicial laws of the Holiness Code are no longer authoritative for Christians (see Westminister [*sic*] Confession XXI.3–5). But it also contains God's permanently binding "moral law"—the prohibition of adultery (Lev. 18.20) and incest (Lev. 20.13) for instance. Moreover, while some parts of the Holiness Code are abrogated by the new covenant in Christ (eating of bloody meat for instance), the New Testament is as firm as the Old in its condemnation of homosexuality. (2) It is true that most Christians today do not believe that those who engage in homosexual activity should be put to death as Leviticus 20.30 prescribes. This is an indication precisely of the fact that they take the Old Testament seriously without using it legalistically. It may also be an indication of the fact that Christians have learned from the Gospel to be more compassionate than those who did not yet know the Gospel. Less severe treatment of homosexual persons in any case does not mean that homosexual practices themselves should not be condemned. (3) We are not told in Leviticus why homosexual practices are condemned there. It may be that the connection of homosexual practices with ancient temple prostitution or with Israel's covenantal expectations were involved. But even apart from this particular historical situation the Holiness Code expresses the fundamental insight of the whole of both the Old and New Testaments that homosexuality is contrary to God's intention for human sexual relationships. Moreover, we can learn from the Holiness Code precisely when we do understand it in the historical context in which it was written that God's people today are to be set apart from other people and are not to order their lives, including their sexual relationships, by the standards which are popular or seem normal to the wider environment in which they live.

How we evaluate all these arguments for and against the authority and relevance of the condemnation of homosexual acts in Leviticus depends not only on the convincingness of their interpretation of this Old Testament material but on whether these interpretations are confirmed or refuted by the study of the New Testament material relating to homosexuality.

B. New Testament

There are three references to homosexuality in the New Testament. In I Timothy 1.8–10 and I Corinthians 6.9–10 homosexual persons are mentioned along with murderers, kidnappers, liars, idolators, adulterers, thieves and drunkards. As in the Leviticus passages, homosexuality receives no special attention here and there is no suggestion that homosexual persons are more sinful than other "immoral persons." I Corinthians 6.9 does, however, include homosexual persons in the list of those who cannot "inherit the kingdom of God."

Romans 1.18–28 deals more specifically with homosexuality, although here too it is not treated as a special problem but is dealt with in the context of a larger question. Paul identifies it here not as a sin but as the result of sin, namely the sin of idolatry. The fundamental sin of the gentiles who are being considered here is that "although they knew God they did not honor him as God" but "exchanged the glory of immortal God for images resembling man or birds or animals or reptiles" and "worshiped and served the creature rather than the Creator." For this reason God "gave them up." He gave them up "in the lust of their hearts to impurity, to the dishonoring of their own bodies among themselves." He gave them up to "dishonorable passions." Both women and men exchanged "natural relations for unnatural" with others of the same sex. Paul's argument is thus that when people's relationship with God is wrong, their relationships with each other, including specifically their sexual relationships, will also be wrong. Homosexuality is not just a moral but a profoundly religious problem.

It is important to remember the broader context in which this condemnation of homosexuality occurs. In the first chapter of Romans Paul is dealing with the sinfulness of gentiles. (Homosexuality may be included here because he shared the Jewish conviction of his time that it is especially characteristic of gentiles.) Chapter two deals with the sinfulness of Jews. (There is no suggestion that the hypocrisy and moral pride of those who "rely on the law" is any less sinful than the sinfulness of the gentiles with their homosexuality.) Chapter three then says of both gentiles and Jews (i.e. of all people) that no one is righteous and that Jews and gentiles alike (those guilty of all the sins mentioned in the first two chapters) are justified by God's grace in Jesus Christ through faith. No one is qualified by his or her righteousness or disqualified by his or her unrighteousness to "inherit the kingdom of God" (I Cor. 6.9). That inheritance is a gift of undeserved and unearned grace offered to all (including those guilty of the homosexual acts condemned in chapter one) despite the nature and extent of their sinfulness.

Paul's position on homosexuality as it is stated in I Corinthians and Romans and reflected in I Timothy has been interpreted by contemporary scholars in both a critical and affirmative direction (similar to the two lines of interpretation we identified in discussing the Leviticus passage).

1. The Critical Interpretation of Paul

Some interpreters believe that Paul's condemnation of homosexuality is not an essential and permanently authoritative part of his apostolic witness but an expression of a traditional Hebraic attitude which shaped the way in which he bore his apostolic witness. They argue that when we respect the witness of Paul to the revelation of God in Jesus Christ, we must question and correct his lingering Jewish understanding of homosexuality in light of the Gospel he himself proclaimed. Moreover, to the extent that Paul's view is shaped not by the Gospel but by the limited knowledge and biases of his time and place in history, that view must be questioned and corrected also in light of what we have learned from modern psychology and sociology. The claim that such a critical evaluation of Paul's position on homosexuality is legitimate and necessary is based on at least four considerations.

(a) In the first place, Paul's lists of vices in Romans and I Corinthians (like the list in I Timothy) are very similar to other categories of vices in Jewish and Graeco-Roman literature of his time such as the writings of Philo, Josephus and the Stoics. This similarity suggests that his condemnation of homosexual acts is rather an unexamined acceptance of the highest Jewish and secular morality of his day than the result of careful reflection on the Gospel he proclaimed and is thus subject to criticism in light of that Gospel.

(b) Secondly, in Romans 1.24ff. Paul connects homosexuality with idolatry. He says that it is the consequence of worshiping and serving the creature rather than the Creator. There is no question that in our day as in Paul's many women and men do make gods of other women and men or of sexual pleasure itself. But are homosexual persons any more prone to such idolatry than heterosexual persons? Why could not homosexual as well as heterosexual love be characterized by a proper acknowledgment of the creatureliness of other human beings and of the creaturely limitation of sexuality in the context of true worship and service of God? Perhaps Paul himself did not witness such non-idolatrous homosexual relationships. Perhaps the prevailing degenerate homosexuality of his time and his ignorance of what we have learned about the causes and nature of homosexuality prevented his conceiving the possibility of such. But do not the witness and lives of Christian homosexual persons in our time as well as our deeper understanding of homosexuality itself lead us to see more clearly than Paul at this point?

(c) Contrary to Paul, Jesus himself did not condemn homosexuality or make heterosexuality a condition for entering into the Kingdom of God. Moreover, Paul's own understanding of the Gospel in Romans 1–3 leads him to proclaim the Good News of God's saving grace to all people, without any discrimination according to sexual orientation.

(d) Finally, Paul argues that homosexuality is not only idolatrous but also "unnatural" (Rom. 1.26f.). Two kinds of arguments are used in evaluating this judgment, one criticizing Paul's understanding of what is natural, the other criticizing not so much Paul himself as the traditional interpretations of him.

Some interpreters criticize Paul's understanding of "natural" sexuality in Romans 1.26f. by relating it to his view of the natural in I Corinthians 11. They point out that in the latter passage Paul expresses some strange ideas about what "nature teaches" (I Cor. 11.14) regarding proper dress and hair styles for women and men. Most Christians today believe that such views reflect not the will of God revealed in nature but social conventions for preserving order, decorum and the good reputation of the Christian community in the near East in the first century. These conventions may have been important for Christians in that time but they are no longer meaningful for us. Paul's acceptance of slavery and his view of the inferior status of women have been criticized the same way. May not Paul's view of the unnaturalness of homosexuality be just as culturally conditioned as his view of the unnaturalness of unveiled women or long-haired men? Are we not just as free—and just as bound—to question his assumptions about homosexuality as his assumptions about slavery and the inferiority of women—especially in light of his own teaching, about the full knowledge of God and his will which are given in Jesus Christ and not in what we can figure out for ourselves by observing nature or creation?

It has also been argued that the people Paul is denouncing in Romans 1.26f. are people who are fundamentally heterosexual but with deliberate perversion choose to "give up" or "exchange" heterosexual for homosexual relationships. For such people homosexual acts are unnatural. Paul does not speak about—and probably did not know about—true homosexual persons who have never been attracted to the opposite sex and for whom it would be unnatural not to have homosexual relationships. He thus leaves room for us to understand unnatural sexual activity to be that which is contrary to one's sexual orientation, whether it is heterosexual or homosexual. Or to put it positively, Paul leaves room for us to believe that natural sexual activity is that which expresses one's true sexual orientation, whether homosexual or heterosexual. This interpretation is of course contrary to the traditional interpretation, and Paul himself may not have envisioned it, but a strict reading of his argument nevertheless allows us to think in this direction.

Those who argue in one way or another for natural homosexuality base their arguments not only on their analysis of Paul's theology but on an interpretation of the broader biblical witness to God's purpose of the life of human beings together as we see it in the Genesis creation narratives and in Jesus Christ. We will return presently to this more general theological argument.

2. The Interpretation in Defense of Paul

Most interpreters in the past have so taken for granted the condemnation of homosexuality in the New Testament that they have not felt it necessary to argue for its validity. In response to contemporary attempts to take a less critical attitude toward homosexuality, the following arguments are made in defense of Paul's and the traditional Christian position:

(a) The fact that the catalogues of sins in the New Testament which condemn homosexuality are similar to those in some Jewish or Graeco-Roman literature of the same period is not an argument against but for their validity. Paul's position gains rather than loses authority because it confirms and is confirmed by non-Christian ethical wisdom. Such agreement proves that all ethically sensitive people are aware that homosexuality is a distortion of right human relationships.

(b) There may indeed be homosexual relationships that are not idolatrous or the consequences of idolatry. But that does not mean that they are legitimate or that Paul's basic argument is wrong. A wrong relationship with God results in wrong human relationships. Even when homosexual people do not worship sexuality as such or sexual partners, homosexuality is still an indication of refusal to honor the Creator and the order he has established for human sexual relatedness.

(c) Jesus did not condemn homosexuality, but his silence does not mean that he approved of it or accepted it. He only spoke of human sexual relationships in the context of marriage between men and women. Moreover, it is of course true that the gospel of God's grace in Christ is offered to all people, including homosexual people. But it is offered to homosexual people as to all others with the requirement of repentance and turning away from sin. Interpreters who argue this way do not always agree in their judgment about what repentance means for homosexual persons. Some seem to say it has to do only with homosexual practices; others, that it has to do with both homosexual activity and homosexual orientation; others speak only of homosexuality in general without making a distinction between practice and orientation. They all agree in emphasizing that in one way or another homosexuality is unnatural and sinful and that the gospel of God's grace in Christ for homosexual persons cannot mean acceptance or approval of their homosexuality.

(d) Paul was right when he said that homosexuality is unnatural. His argument about what is natural in dress and hair-style may sound strange to us (through we may still learn something from it concerning the importance of preserving order, decorum and the good reputation of the Christian community). But that issue is clearly of a different nature from the issue of homosexuality. The social conventions of his time may have influenced his ideas about styles of dress and hair arrangement, but his position on homosexuality is based on God's intention for human sexual relationships in all times and places.

Those who support Paul on homosexuality do not agree in their evaluation of the parallel drawn between his position on this issue and his position on slavery and the inferior status of women. Few would want to argue for the acceptance of slavery today, but some believe that his view of what is the natural and God-willed place and conduct of women in the Church is as authoritative for us today as his understanding of what is natural and God-willed in sexual relationships. Others believe that we can distinguish between these issues. Paul's own statements about slavery and women in other passages (as well as the attitudes and actions of Jesus himself) give us ground for rethinking the issue of slavery and women, but neither Jesus nor Paul gives us ground for such re-evaluation of the rejection of homosexuality.

In opposition to the argument that Romans 1.26f. says that the practice of homosexuality is unnatural only for those who are heterosexually oriented, the argument must be that Paul means to say that homosexuality itself is unnatural and against the united biblical witness to the purpose of God's created order.

Those who defend as well as those who criticize Paul's position on homosexuality appeal to the broader base of God's creative and redemptive purpose for human sexuality in general. We turn now to summarize their arguments on this more general level.

C. The Total Biblical Witness

The differences of interpretation which emerge from reflection of those passages in the Old and New Testaments dealing specifically with homosexuality are not resolved by asking what Scripture as a whole teaches about human sexuality in general. On the contrary, the same differences of opinion emerge in this broader context. What reflection at this level can do is help us articulate the fundamental biblical-theological issue which underlies all the individual texts and various interpretations we have discussed. The fundamental question is whether or not

God's creative and redemptive purpose for human sexuality relates exclusively to male-female relatedness.

1. *The argument for exclusively male-female relatedness.* The classical Christian position is that God created human beings with a biological (and perhaps also psychological) sexual differentiation so that the distinction between male and female is an essential part of every persons's [*sic*] human identity. But God also saw that it is not good for human beings to be alone (Gen. 2.18). His purpose in creating them male and female was not only to distinguish them from each other but to enable them to fulfill their humanity in mutually loving relationship with each other. This God-created sexual differentiation and sexual relatedness is most profoundly expressed in the faithful and monogamous marital union of men and women (though even apart from sexual intimacy and marriage men and women are still distinguished from each other as male and female and should relate to each other as such). Sometimes the Church (especially in Protestantism) has spoken and acted as if unmarried people (whether never married, divorced or widowed) are less than fully human beings. Sometimes it has spoken and acted as if men and women who do not produce children are also less than fully human beings and are perhaps even guilty of disobeying God's command "to be fruitful and multiply." When the Church has thus made marriage and parenthood a condition of human fulfillment, it has contradicted its own orthodox theology which asserts that the humanity of Jesus is the perfect norm of all genuine humanity though he was neither married nor a parent. Even when the Church has avoided tying genuine *humanity* to marriage and parenthood, however, it has maintained that according to God's creative purpose the physical expression of human *sexuality* can properly take place only in the heterosexual relationship of marriage.

When we move from the Genesis account of creation to the New Testament, we see that Jesus did not describe new life in the Kingdom of God in terms of the male-female relationship. He suggested that marriage (though not necessarily sexuality) will end with the coming of the Kingdom (Mk. 12.25). He taught that the decisive relationship for life in the Kingdom is the relationship of people not with the opposite sex but with God and neighbors. Nevertheless Jesus affirmed God's original intention for males and females to be united in monogamous, faithful marriage (Mk. 10.2ff.). He blessed marriage (John 2.1ff.). In the context of a discussion of homosexuality it is noteworthy that he did not reject or avoid contact with women but counted women as well as men among his close friends and followers.

For Paul too the new humanity or new creation we hope for in Christ and already experience in the present by the power of the Holy Spirit, is not tied to the male-female relationship. In Christ all are one; there is neither male nor female (Gal. 3.28). In I Corinthians 7 Paul expresses the opinion that in view of the coming end of all things it is better to be unmarried because sexual desire and the responsibilities of marriage make it difficult to be concerned about the "affairs of the Lord." Nevertheless, even in this chapter Paul affirms the legitimacy of sex and marriage, recognizing that whether married or single "each has his own special gift from God," and should "lead the life which the Lord has assigned him." In Ephesians 5.21ff. he chose the husband-wife relationship to speak of the relationship between Christ and the Church. We have already noted how he views heterosexuality as the "natural" expression of physical human relatedness.

According to the traditional interpretation, then, the New Testament as well as the Old recognizes only male-female relatedness as the proper expression of human sexuality. Especially in the New Testament physical sexual activity is considered good (within the bounds of marriage) but not necessary.

2. *The argument for sexual relatedness not limited to the male-female distinction.* Some contemporary theologians and many homosexual Christians believe that biblical teachings about the male-female relationship should not be narrowly interpreted as the expression of God's will for heterosexual relationships only. The biblical understanding of the distinction and relationship between male and female is the prototype and example of all truly human relationships, non-sexual as well as sexual, homosexual as well as heterosexual.

From the biblical teaching about the distinction between male and female we learn to acknowledge and respect the God-created uniqueness and individuality—the "otherness"—of every human being. We also learn that truly human relatedness is possible only when this distinctiveness of the other is honored and preserved, not dissolved into an undifferentiated sameness. True relatedness means the togetherness of people who are *different* from each other. This distinctiveness in relationship is indeed reflected in the male-female relationship. But why should it be *limited* to male-female relatedness? Is it not also the prototype of the right relationship also between people of different races, cultures, nationalities and the like? Why should it not also be the prototype of right homosexual relationships? Homosexual relationships are admittedly relationships between people of the same sex, but the sexual distinction is not the only way in which people are distinguished from each other. So long as (and to the extent that) a homosexual relationship is not in fact the attempt to deny or escape but the attempt to realize encounter with someone recognized to be genuinely "other," why could it not be authentically human? Cannot there be mutual honor and respect of the uniqueness and individuality of the other in homosexual as well as in heterosexual relationships, and thus in one way as well as the other the realization of the unity-with-distinction which reflects God's creative purpose for the life of human beings together?

Those who argue that the God-intended *distinction* between the partners in male-female relationships can also be preserved in homosexual relationships also argue that the quality of God-willed *relatedness* in the one can also be expressed in the other. "It is not good that man should be alone" means that God created human beings so that they cannot be human in lonely isolation, self-sufficiency and autonomy. He created them to be persons-in-relationship whose essential humanity is expressed in mutual need for one another and fulfilled in mutual commitment to love and help one another. Moreover, since God created human beings as physical creatures, not as disembodied souls or spirits or minds, he intended this mutual need, commitment, love and help to be expressed in physical intimacy. The biblical account of God's creation of male and female *illustrates* and *manifests* this being-in-relationship. But why should we conclude that such being-in-relationship can be fulfilled only in a male-female relationship? Is it any better for homosexual than for heterosexual persons to be alone? May not homosexual as well as heterosexual relationships express the mutual need, commitment, love and help God intended for all human beings? If homosexual persons too have been created physical sexual beings, why should not their mutuality also be expressed in physical desire and love-making? If we deny homosexual persons the only kind of deep personal relatedness possible for them, do we not cut them off from the very thing that constitutes their God-created and God-willed humanity? Those who argue this way emphasize that they are not arguing for "only" physical relatedness, or for casual or promiscuous sexuality, any more than those who speak of God-willed male-female relatedness argue for such. Standards such as permanence, unreserved self-giving and faithfulness which apply to right heterosexual relationships also apply to right homosexual relationships.

If God created human beings so that their humanity is being-in-relationship, and if this relatedness can be expressed homosexually as well as heterosexually, what then does Christ mean for homosexual persons? Just what he means for heterosexual persons. He died and rose again and lives for homosexual persons too. He is also their Savior and Lord. To them too are directed all the warnings and promises, judgment and grace, of the Gospel. They too are called to faith and repentance. They too are forgiven, accepted, justified by grace through faith. They too are given new life in Christ by the Holy Spirit and are called to live it out faithfully and obediently in every area of life. They too are invited to participation in the community of God's people—to hear the word, receive the sacraments, share in the fellowship, join the Church's mission in the world. In short, they too may participate in and hope for the new humanity Jesus Christ brings and promises to all those who follow him and live in his company. And all this happens not as homosexual persons are called out of their homosexuality but as they learn to live faithful and obedient Christian lives within it.

The fundamental theological issue underlying the Church's discussion of homosexuality is whether this is a legitimate and convincing interpretation of the meaning of creation and redemption for human sexuality. When the discussion reaches this level, our problem is no longer one of understanding but one of decision. The alternatives before us are clear. Which should we choose?

V. Alternatives Before the Church

At least three broad positions (with variations in the first two) for understanding homosexuality and dealing with homosexual persons emerge from the clinical data we have summarized in sections I and II, from the theological and ethical presuppositions we have summarized in section III and from the interpretations of the biblical material we have summarized in section IV. It is clear that while some of the elements in the three positions can be combined, we are presented here not with equally valid options but with real alternatives which call for decision.

1. *Some Christians believe that homosexuality is a sickness or arrested psychosexual development.* (For the purpose of our discussion we can combine these two clinical diagnoses though they are different and result in different attitudes toward homosexual persons.) Homosexual persons should be understood as sick people who need to be cured or as immature people who need to be enabled to grow into the capacity for mature heterosexual relationships. The Church should encourage (require?) homosexual persons who want to participate in its fellowship and ministry to seek psychiatric help and the help of God's grace to be healed of this sickness, or to be freed from the crippling influences which have retarded their psychosexual growth, so that they might become heterosexual. The Church should also offer its support and help to people who are struggling to overcome their homosexuality.

If the Church should adopt this position and carry it out responsibly, it would be aware of the increasing difficulty of overcoming this disease or handicap the closer a person is to an exclusively homosexual orientation or condition. It would also take into consideration the distinction between homosexual activity and homosexual orientation. It would then have three possible ways of implementing this basic stance:

(a) The Church could refuse to accept into its fellowship and ministry those who cannot or will not change their abnormal sexual orientation. In this case it would have to be prepared to answer the question why and to what extent psychological health or wholeness or maturity is a prerequisite for participation in the Church's life and work, and on what grounds it excludes people with this psychological problem when it is willing to include those who are psychologically sick or retarded in other ways. It would also have to come to terms with Jesus' statement that he came precisely for those who are sick and not for those who are well (Mk. 2.17).

(b) The Church could accept into its fellowship and ministry those who give up all homosexual activity, even though they cannot or will not change their homosexual orientation. In this case it would have to struggle with the problem of requiring a split between what homosexual persons are and how they live, and with the consequence of asking them to give up the only expression of sexuality possible for them.

(c) Having encouraged or required homosexual persons to seek to be cured of their sickness or freed of their handicap in every possible way, the Church could receive into its fellowship and ministry those for whom heterosexuality is impossible on the condition that they live out their homosexuality in an ethically responsible way within the limited possibilities of their psychosexual orientation. (See 2.c below.) Both for its own protection and for the protection of homosexual persons themselves, the Church could then consider whether it would be wise (with proper discretion and sensitivity to the feelings and needs of all involved) to make some policies about the kinds of responsibilities and opportunities which should be open to homosexual people in its fellowship. If it chose this alternative, the Church would have to be careful that it did not prematurely encourage homosexual people to accept their sickness or crippled condition and cease the struggle for psychosexual health, wholeness and maturity.

The fundamental assumption behind all three of these alternatives is rejected by those who do not accept the clinical diagnosis of homosexuality as abnormal in one way or another, by those who believe on biblical-theological grounds that it is not primarily a manifestation of psychological disorder but of sin, and by those who believe that responsible homosexuality may be both psychologically and theologically justified as one form of healthy and whole sexuality.

2. *Some Christians believe that homosexuality is sinful.* Homosexual people need to repent of and give up their homosexuality. They may indeed have psychological problems, and when they do they should be encouraged and supported as they seek appropriate psychological help. But even if some homosexual persons are or become well-adjusted in the homosexuality and even if behavioral scientists should reach the consensus that homosexuality in itself is not a sickness or the manifestation of psychosexual immaturity, the Church must still understand it as a sinful distortion of the sexuality God intends for human beings. The Church, therefore, cannot under any circumstances approve of homosexuality. Its task is in word and deed to enable homosexual people to hear the gospel of Christ which at once condemns their sinfulness, assures them of God's forgiveness, and promises them new life according to God's will in the area of sexuality as in all other areas of life.

Responsible application of this position would also involve awareness of the increasing difficulty of change the closer a person is to an exclusively homosexual orientation and consideration of the distinction between homosexual activity and homosexual orientation. It would then have three possible procedures of implementation similar to those mentioned above, though the problems connected with them are different when the point of view is theological rather than merely clinical. (In principle the clinical and theological positions are not necessarily mutually exclusive but could be so formulated that they mutually support and supplement each other.)

(a) The Church could refuse to accept into its fellowship and ministry those who do not repent of and give up their sinful homosexual orientation to become heterosexual. In this case it would have to be willing to accept responsibility for rejecting from participation in its life and work—and excluding from the promises of the Gospel—not only those who willfully refuse to become heterosexual but also those who with all good will and in dependence on every resource of divine and human help cannot become heterosexual. It would also have to be prepared to answer the question why it rejects and excludes people with this sinful disposition when it accepts and includes people with other sinful dispositions—people, for instance, who are envious, greedy, covetous, haughty, filled with malice, etc. (sins which in Romans 1.28ff. and I Corinthians 6.9ff. Paul mentions along with the sin of homosexuality without suggesting that it is more sinful than these other sins). Finally, the Church would also have to acknowledge that at the same time it is also rejecting and excluding from the promises of the Gospel those in its membership who are unrecognized and non-practicing homosexual persons.

(b) The Church could accept into its fellowship and ministry those who repent of and give up homosexual activity even though they may not be able to change their homosexual orientation. Leaving to God judgment about what lies in the hearts and minds of people, the Church would concern itself only with what they do. In this case it would have to be careful that it did not fall into a very superficial view of sin and repentance, which the New Testament teaches us involves not only external deeds but also the internal motivations and desires of the heart. It would also have to be careful that it did not give the impression that it encourages and approves of hypocrisy both on the part of homosexual persons themselves and on the part of a Church satisfied only with external change. It would have to be very careful not to encourage legalistic self-righteousness (or perhaps unexpressed hopelessness) on the part of others in the Church who may be homosexual "in their hearts" but have never engaged in homosexual activity. Finally, it would have to be willing to stand by the serious consequences of demanding celibacy of those for whom homosexual love is the only possibility of sexual expression.

(c) Having encouraged and helped homosexual persons in every way to repent and become heterosexual, the Church could receive into its fellowship and ministry those for whom heterosexuality is an impossibility if they commit themselves to the Christian faith and life within the limitations of the kind of human sexuality and sexual expression that is possible for them. It would consider both the homosexual orientation and homosexual practices to be sinful, but practicing homosexual persons (like those guilty of other sins) would not be excluded from the Church and promises of the gospel. They would be urged to continue to struggle with their particular temptations in the fellowship and with the support of other Christians in the Christian community, depending just like other sinners in the Church on God's forgiving and renewing grace. The Church would not approve of homosexuality but would accept homosexual persons, inviting them and requiring them to live out their form of sexuality in an ethically responsible way. So, for instance, homosexual persons would be encouraged to avoid situations in which the danger of temptation is great, to develop the non-sexual sides of life and keep sexual activity in proportion to other parts of life, to relate to other people of the opposite sex and of the same sex in a human (not just genital) way, to reject promiscuity and to develop a permanent relationship with another person which is not exploitative and impersonal but involves mutual respect and love.

If it choses [*sic*] this alternative, the Church would have to struggle with the problem of accepting in practice what it rejects in theory. It would have to be careful that it did not too easily give up on the renewing power of God's grace, thus allowing the condemned homosexual persons to settle into a sexual orientation and way of life less than the fully human sexual relatedness God wills for all people. It would also have to deal with the practical and pastoral problems involved in integrating homosexual persons into the life and work of the Christian community, exercising realistic and compassionate concern both for homosexual persons themselves and for others.

The fundamental assumption behind all three of these alternatives is rejected by those who for psychological and/or theological reasons do not believe that homosexuality and its practices are sinful in themselves. The last alternative, which at first glance seems most open to compromise, is as objectionable as the first two to homosexual persons (and others who agree with them) who cannot accept a position which they believe patronizingly only "allows" them "nevertheless" to participate in the Church and thus condemn, though benevolently, a way of life they consider good, natural and God-willed for them.

3. *Some Christians believe that homosexuality is a legitimate variety of human sexuality.* For homosexual persons it is just as natural, normal and pleasing to God as heterosexuality is for heterosexual persons. Those who hold this position believe that the Church must therefore accept homosexuality as a legitimate form of sexuality and welcome homosexual persons into its fellowship and ministry without any reservations or qualifications except those concerning faith and obedience which are applicable to everyone else.

If the Church should responsibly adopt this position, it would acknowledge also in this case that a homosexual orientation is increasingly difficult to change the closer one comes to an exclusively homosexual orientation, and also in this case it would support the efforts of homosexual persons who want to and are able to become heterosexual. But it would not consider such change either necessary or desirable for those who cannot or will not change their homosexual orientation. Moreover, the Church would also in this case take into consideration the connection between homosexual orientation and sexual expression. It would consider homosexual activity by people who are not genuinely homosexual in orientation to be sinful and/or sick or distorted, and help such people to overcome the self-destructive contradiction between their true psychosexual orientation and their sexual activity. It would further acknowledge that genuinely homosexual persons may express their particular form of sexuality in sinful and/or sick or immature ways, and help to free them of their sin and/or heal their psychologically disordered lives. But that would mean to help them become not heterosexual but homosexual persons who live out their homosexuality in a healthy Christian way.

If the Church should take this affirmative attitude toward homosexuality and homosexual persons, it would have to be sure that it is able to recognize and define "genuine" homosexuality. It would have to be certain that the most accepting attitude toward *homosexuality* is the most living and helpful attitude toward homosexual *persons* and that it would not be encouraging a way of life that handicaps or destroys the possibility of homosexual persons achieving the full humanity they quite properly seek for themselves. In other words, it would have to be sure that it could justify its position theologically and psychologically. Finally, it would have to struggle with the educational and pastoral problems involved in taking a position so radically different from the traditional Christian position on this issue.

This position is of course rejected by those who do not believe that the scientific clinical evidence warrants such an unreserved affirmation of homosexuality and by those who do not believe that even a non-legalistic historical and theological interpretation of Scripture supports it.

VI. Guidelines

Variations of each of the three basic positions we have outlined are chosen by faithful Christians who find the problems involved in their particular position easier to deal with than those of other positions. Since homosexuality itself is such a complex phenomenon and since every homosexual person is a unique human being, it may be that no one theoretical position could be formulated which would be adequate to deal with every form of homosexuality and every homosexual person. All serious Christians will be compelled to reject one or another of these positions. But in view of the complexity of the issue, the disagreement among Christians and the variety in the character and experience of homosexual persons themselves, it seems unwise at this time to propose any one position as *the* position of our Church. We therefore offer some general guidelines which have emerged from our study. They do not solve the problem but they should help individual Christians, church sessions and presbyteries make their decisions with more understanding, compassion and responsibility as they deal with particular homosexual persons in concrete situations.

1. *Concerning those who make decisions about homosexuality and homosexual persons*

a. Informed and responsible decisions can be made only with the help of experts in the behavioral sciences who have insight into the psychological and sociological influences which cause homosexuality and shape the psychosexual orientation and behavior of homosexual people.

b. Sincere desire to know the will of God for homosexual persons means openness to the possibility that what we think we already know may need to be corrected by a fresh listening for God's will as it is made known in Jesus Christ by his Spirit both through Scripture and through brother and sister Christians who may hear a different word when they seek the will of the same God in the same Christ through the same Scripture, guided by the same Spirit.

c. Genuine concern to understand and minister to homosexual persons requires open and compassionate listening to what they have to say about themselves, their experiences, their feelings and their way of life. Like all other persons, homosexual persons are best known and understood through personal encounter, not through theories, second-hand reports and speculation.

d. The "homosexual problem" is also a heterosexual problem, the problem of the ignorance, fear, anxiety and prejudice of heterosexual people when they encounter homosexual people. Genuine concern to understand and minister to homosexual persons requires willingness on the part of heterosexual persons to let themselves be instructed, judged, corrected, called to repentance and given a new spirit of justice and love in dealing with those who are different from them.

e. Those in the Church who make judgments about homosexuality and homosexual persons will make their decisions with more compassion and humility when they examine themselves and the Church to discover what part they have played in the psychological and cultural conditioning that helps create homosexuality. What has the Church done or not done to influence right relationships between husbands and wives, parents and children? In its ministry to children and youth to what extent has the Church left unchallenged or itself encouraged distorted views of masculinity and femininity, created or paid no attention to the loneliness and insecurity of those who do not fit the expected masculine or feminine roles of our culture?

2. *Concerning homosexual persons as human beings*

a. There is as much diversity in the expression of homosexuality as in the expression of heterosexuality. It is as false to say what "all" homosexual persons are like and how they live as to say what "all" heterosexual persons are like and how they live. Like every heterosexual person, each homosexual person can be understood and ministered to only as the unique human being he or she is, with his or her unique problems and needs, limitations and possibilities, weaknesses and strengths.

b. Like heterosexual persons, homosexual persons cannot be understood exclusively in terms of their sexual orientation. Sexuality is no more "all there is" to a person in one case than in the other. Like heterosexual persons, homosexual persons may be responsible in their chosen vocations, generous and loving in personal relationships, diligent in striving for justice and peace in the social order, committed to the Christian faith and life. Because they have often experienced being hurt, rejected and discriminated against, homosexual persons may in fact be especially sensitive to the needs, hurts and feelings of others, and especially aware of their need for the comfort and strength offered by the Christian gospel.

c. Homosexual persons in general are no more threatening to the welfare of society and the Church than are heterosexual persons in general. Society and the Church legitimately seek to protect their welfare from those homosexual persons as from those heterosexual persons who do threaten their welfare. For the sake of those who are sexually attracted to young people as well as for the sake of the young themselves, children and youth are especially to be protected from homosexual as from heterosexual pedophilia.

d. Whether homosexuality is understood as sin, psychological disorder or simply a variation of sexuality, all homosexual persons are to be respected as human beings created in the image of God. Persecution, contempt, mockery and condescending pity are inhuman and unchristian in relation to homosexual persons as in relation to all other human beings. Jesus' command that we love our neighbors applies to our neighbors who are homosexual as well as to those who are heterosexual.

3. *Concerning theological and ethical judgments*

a. Scripture teaches us that all of us are not only what we do but also what we feel, desire and think. A legalistic concentration on external actions which ignores internal motivations and dispositions is as wrong in dealing with homosexuality as in dealing with any other ethical problem. Those who make responsible judgments about homosexuality and homosexual persons cannot assume that only those are homosexual who engage in homosexual activity or that those who no longer engage in it have forsaken homosexuality. On the other hand, human beings, who cannot see into the hearts of others, must be careful about judging anyone on any other basis than what he or she says about himself or herself and how he or she acts.

b. Homosexual persons are as responsible as heterosexual persons for their sexual behavior and the quality of their relationships with other people. Promiscuity, sexual self-gratification which uses another person as an object, sexual seduction which manipulates another and sexual violence are as wrong for homosexual as for heterosexual persons.

c. Full humanity and genuine personal relationships do not require explicit sexual activity either for heterosexual or for homosexual persons.

d. The psychosexual orientation of homosexual persons (like that of heterosexual persons) is not simply the result of their deciding and choosing but to a smaller or greater extent the result of complex and deep-rooted psychological and sociological factors which shaped their sexual orientation long before they were able to choose, and which continue to shape their choosing. Homosexual persons therefore cannot simply "decide" to change their sexual orientation even if they will. Such change becomes increasingly difficult the closer they approach an exclusive homosexual orientation and may be impossible for some.

e. Homosexual persons (like heterosexual persons) should not use "nature" or "fate" or "chance" or "my parents" or "society" as an excuse for hopeless or self-satisfied resignation which refuses to take responsibility for the kind of persons they are and can become.

f. When the possibility of change in psychosexual orientation is considered, the power of God's grace must be taken into account as well as the power of psychological and sociological influences and the power of self-determination. It must be remembered that God is free and not compelled to do what we think or earnestly desire that he should. Moreover, God's grace may mean his comforting and sustaining people in the given circumstances of their lives as well as his delivering them from those circumstances.

g. The Church should require no more moral perfection or psychological health and maturity of homosexual than of heterosexual persons.

h. The Church is called to bear witness to the justice of the Kingdom of God by standing for justice in human society. Whether or not Christians accept or approve of homosexuality itself, they should stand for just treatment of homosexual persons as well as all other persons in our society. They should advocate and defend for homosexual persons also the civil liberties, equal rights and protection under the law from social and economic discrimination which are due all other citizens.

APPENDIX A

The 1972 General Assembly of the Presbyterian Church U.S. received the following resolution:

"Whereas, there is in our culture today a great deal of discussion about homosexuality, both with approval and disapproval; and,

"Whereas, the Bible speaks clearly for every Christian to understand the divine will on this subject (Romans 1:26–27):

> 'For this cause God gave them up unto vile affection: for even their women did change the natural use into that which is against nature. And likewise also the men, leaving the natural use of the women, burned in their lust one toward another; men with men working that which is unseemly, and receiving in themselves that recompense of their error which was meet'

and,

"Whereas, there seems to be confusion in the minds of many persons in our denomination because of what other religious bodies and periodicals have said and done on the subject; therefore,

"Be it resolved that this General Assembly reaffirms its conviction that homosexual behavior is a grievous sin, that marriages (so called) between two of the same sex are contrary to the divine plan and under divine wrath (Roman [*sic*] 1:27); but

"Be it further resolved that the Church express its deep love and compassion for all those struggling with this problem as other spiritual problems and offer its Christian help and counsel to assist them in making normal and wholesome adjustments to life."

This resolution was referred to the Council on Church and Society which subsequently referred it to the Council on Theology and Culture in the following manner:

"The 112th General Assembly (1972) referred to the Council Commissioner Resolution 5 concerning homosexuality, with the request that the Council submit recommendations to a subsequent General Assembly (1972 *Minutes,* p. 182). Council Recommendation 4 requests that the General Assembly refer this issue to the new Council on Theology and Culture.

APPENDIX B

From the *Minutes* of the 116th General Assembly (1976), Overture from Fayetteville Presbytery:

"Whereas, the 112th General Assembly of the Presbyterian Church in the United States received and referred to the Council on Church and Society a resolution calling for General Assembly to 'reaffirm its convictin [*sic*] that homo-sexual behavior is a grievous sin' while expressing 'its deep love and compas-sion for all those struggling with this problem as other spiritual problems, and offer its Christian help and counsel to assist them in making normal and whole-some adjustments to life', and

Whereas, the 113th General Assembly, acting on recommendation of the Council on Church and Society, referred this matter to the Council on Theology and Culture, requesting recommendations concerning this matter be made to a subsequent General Assembly, and

Whereas, the 114th General Assembly received the report from the Council on Theology and Culture that 'the Council is in the process of designing and orga-nizing a task force in this area', and

Whereas, the 115th General Assembly granted the Council on Theology and Culture additional time to continue their study, and

Whereas, such delay in speaking to the issue of homosexual behavior can but lead to confusion and possible misunderstanding as to the attitude of the Presby-terian Church in the United States toward homosexual behavior,

Therefore, the Presbytery of Fayetteville overtures the 116th General Assem-bly of the Presbyterian Church in the United States to adopt the following state-ment concerning homosexuality as the official position of the Presbyterian Church in the United States:

Homosexuality

"Believing 'the Holy Scriptures of the Old and New Testaments are the word of God, the only rule of faith and obedience' (The Larger Catechism, A. 3), and knowing that authorities in the field of human behavior often contradict each other and are, at best, but secondary guides to the ordering of human behavior, the 116th General Assembly of the Presbyterian Church in the United States must base its decisions concerning the practice of homosexuality on Scripture alone.

"The Old Testament witnesses strongly against the practice of homosexuality. The seventh commandment, 'Thou shalt not commit adultery', has been inter-preted by the Larger Catechism (A.139) to include forbidding 'sodomy and all unnatural lusts'. Sodomy, which is a homosexual practice, received its name from the biblical account of the fall of Sodom and Gomorrah (Genesis 19), as the men of Sodom demanded of Lot that his male visitors be given to them that they might 'know' them. The term 'to know' is interpreted to mean 'to know sexually'. Lot's offer to give his own daughters to the men instead of the visitors indicates the truth of this interpretation. Jude 6–7 speaks of the fate of Sodom and Gomorrah in these terms:

'And the angels that did not keep their own position but left their proper dwelling have been kept in eternal chains in the nether gloom until the judgment of the great day; just as Sodom and Gomorrah and the surrounding cities, which likewise acted immorally and indulged in the unnatural lust, served as an example by undergoing a punishment of eternal fire.'

"Leviticus 18:22 condemns the practice of homosexuality: 'You shall not lie with a male as with a women [sic]; it is an abomination.' Leviticus 20:13 underscores the seriousness of the offense: 'If a man lies with a male as with a woman, both of them have committed an abomination; they shall be put to death, their blood is upon them.'

"Even as the Old Testament condemns the practice of homosexuality, so does the New. Romans 1:24–27 calls homosexual acts 'unnatural', 'shameless' and 'error':

'Therefore God gave them up in the lust of their hearts to impurity, to the dishonoring of their bodies among themselves, because they exchanged the truth about God for a lie and worshiped and served the creature rather than the Creator, who is blessed forever! Amen. For this reason God gave them up to the dishonorable passions. Their women exchanged natural relations for unnatural, and the men likewise gave up natural relations with women and were consumed with passion for one another, men committing shameless acts with men and receiving in their own persons the due penalty for their error.'

"I Corinthians 6:9–10 classifies the homosexual with the 'unrighteous who will not inherit the kingdom of God', stating:

'Do you not know that the unrighteous will not inherit the kingdom of God? Do not be deceived; neither the immoral, nor idolators, nor adulters [sic], nor homosexuals, nor thieves, nor the greedy, nor drunkards, nor revilers, nor robbers, will inherit the kingdom of God.'

"I Timothy 1:8–11 also places the sodomite in very unhealthy company, and declares that lot as 'contrary to sound doctrine':

'Now we know that the law is good, if anyone uses it lawfully, understanding this, that the law is not laid down for the just but for the lawless and disobedient, for the ungodly and sinners, for the unholy and profane, for murderers of fathers and murderers of mothers, for manslayers, immoral persons, sodomites, kidnappers, liars, perjurers, and whatever else is contrary to sound doctrine, in accordance with the glorious gospel of the blessed God with which I have been entrusted.'

"Although there are other passages in Scripture which condemn the practice of homosexuality by implication, these illustrations are sufficient to point to an unequivocal biblical condemnation of homosexuality. The practice of homosexuality should be shunned by the Christian as he or she would shun adultery, fornication, robbery, manslaughter, and the other sins specifically condemned in Scripture.

"However, we must remember that, although homosexuality is condemned by Scripture, the Gospel of Jesus Christ is open to the homosexual on the same basis as it is for any other sinner. John 3:16 makes no exceptions as it begins, 'For God so loved the world. . .' This most certainly includes the homosexual in the same measure as the self-righteous, the hypocrite, and the gossip, to name but a few who are tempted to judge the homosexual. While I Corinthians 6:9–10 condemns homosexuality along with other sins, verse 11 says to the Corinthians, 'And such were some of you. But you were washed, you were sanctified, you were justified in the name of the Lord Jesus Christ and in the Spirit of our God.' Therefore, the Christian is bound to extend the Gospel of Jesus Christ to the homosexual on the same basis the Gospel should be extended to everyone else. Our attitude toward the homosexual should be to 'hate every trace of their sin while being merciful (and loving in the sense of I Corinthians 13) to them as sinners' (Jude 23, Living Bible). The Gospel is to be offered, and help given, that the homosexual might be redeemed by the blood of Christ and the practice of homosexuality forsaken.

"It must be understood that the practice of homosexuality is to be forsaken before Church membership or Church office is accepted, just as a person is expected to give up fornication, adultery, lawlessness, or any other practice which is condemned and forbidden by Scripture. The homosexual is to be helped in his or her understanding of this and assured that, 'Therefore if any one is in Christ, he is a new creation; the old has passed away, behold the new has come' (I Corinthians 6:17), thus offering the hope of a new life in Christ Jesus.

"In conclusion, the General Assembly of the Presbyterian Church in the United States affirms its conviction that homosexual behavior is a grievous sin according to the Scriptures, expresses its deep love and compassion for all who struggle with this problem, as with all spiritual problems, and offers the help of all its counseling resources to assist them in making normal and wholesome adjustments to life in Jesus Christ.'"

Action of the 116th General Assembly (1976) as follows:

(a) That the 116th General Assembly express its sense of urgency concerning this matter, with the request that this study become a priority item with the Council on Theology and Culture in anticipation if at all possible, of a completed report to the 117th General Assembly.

(b) That commissioners to the 116th General Assembly who wish to express their feelings, concerns, and viewpoints in regard to this issue be encouraged to do so, in writing, to the Council on Theology and Culture at their earliest opportunity; and that the Council on Theology and Culture be instructed to give full and serious attention to each expressed viewpoint in their deliberating and drafting of a completed report.

(c) That the Council on Theology and Culture be instructed by the 116th General Assembly to give thorough consideration to other denominational statements expressing their concerns and viewpoints on this issue, especially those statements of other members of our Reformed tradition such as the 188th General Assembly of the UPCUSA and the statement issued in 1970 by the Lutheran Church in America.

Recommendation concerning the Fayetteville Overture:

That Overture 76–55 from the Presbytery of Fayetteville regarding a statement concerning homosexuality be answered by referring it to the Council on Theology and Culture as a matter of concern and information. (PCUS General Assembly *Minutes,* 1976, p. 217)

BIBLIOGRAPHY

Bailey, Derrick S. *Homosexuality and the Western Christian Tradition.* London: Longmans, Green and Co., 1955.

Barth, Karl, *Church Dogmatics* III/4. Edinburgh: T. and T. Clark, 1961.

Bieber, Irving et al. *Homosexuality: A Psychoanalytic Study.* New York: Basic Books, 1962.

Cappon, Daniel. *Toward an Understanding of Homosexuality.* Englewood Cliffs, N. J.: Prentice-Hall, 1965.

Cole, William Graham. *Sex and Love in the Bible.* New York: Association Press, 1959.

Heron, Alastair, ed. *Towards a Quaker View of Sex.* London: Friends Home Service Committee, 1963.

Hettlinger, Richard. *Sex Isn't That Simple: New Sexuality on the Campus.* New York: Seabury Press, 1974.

Hooker, Evelyn. "Homosexuality," in Elizabeth S. and William H. Genne, eds., *Foundations for Christian Family Policy.* New York: National Council of Churches, 1961, pp. 166–89.

———. "Male Homosexuals and Their Worlds," in Judd Marmor, ed., *Sexual Inversion: The Multiple Roots of Homosexuality.* New York: Basic Books, 1965, pp. 83–107.

Jones, H. Kimball. *Toward a Christian Understanding of the Homosexual.* New York: Association Press, 1966.

Kinsey, Alfred C. et al. *Sexual Behavior in the Human Female.* Philadelphia: W. B. Saunders Co., 1953.

———. *Sexual Behavior in the Human Male.* Philadelphia: W. B. Saunders Co., 1948.

Marmor, Judd, ed. *Sexual Inversion: The Multiple Roots of Homosexuality.* New York: Basic Books, 1975 [*sic*].

Martin, Del and Lyon, Phyllis. *Lesbian Women.* New York: Bantom [*sic*], 1972.

Money, John and Zubin, J. *Contemporary Sexual Behavior.* Baltimore: Johns Hopkins, 1973.

———. *Sexual Signatures: On Being a Man or Woman.* Boston: Little Brown, 1975.

Perry, Troy. *The Lord Is My Shepherd and He Knows I'm Gay.* Los Angeles: Nash, 1972.

Pittenger, Norman. *Time for Consent? A Christian's Approach to Homosexuality.* London: SCM Press, 1967.

Smedes, Lewis B. *Sex for Christians: The Limits and Liberties of Sexual Living.* Grand Rapids: Eerdman's [*sic*], 1976.

Thielicke, Helmut. *The Ethics of Sex.* New York: Harper and Row, 1964.

Weinberg, Martin and Williams, Colin. *Male Homosexuals: Their Problems and Adaptations.* New York: Oxford Press, 1974.

Weltge, Ralph W., ed. *The Same Sex.* Philadelphia: Pilgrim Press, 1969.

OTHER DENOMINATIONAL STATEMENTS REGARDING HOMOSEXUALITY

From: "A Synoptic of Recent Denominational Statements on Sexuality" Second Edition, compiled by William H. Genne, National Council of Churches.

Lutheran Church in America: Statement on Sex, Marriage and Family, 1970 Scientific research has not been able to provide conclusive evidence regarding the causes of homosexuality. Nevertheless, homosexuality is viewed biblically as a departure from the heterosexual structure of God's creation. Persons who engage in homosexual behavior are sinners only as are all other persons—alienated from

God and neighbor. However, they are often the special and undeserving victims of prejudice and discrimination in law, law enforcement, cultural mores, and congregational life. In relation to this area of concern, the sexual behavior of freely consenting adults in private is not an appropriate subject for legislation or police action. It is essential to see such persons as entitled to understanding and justice in church and community.

Moravian Church in America: 1974
Resolved that the Moravian Church reaffirm its open welcome to all people by specifically recognizing that the homosexual is also under God's care, and be it further resolved that Moravian congregations will extend an invitation to all persons to join us in a common search for wholeness before God and persons and be it further resolved that as Christians recognizing our common sinfulness and the miracle of God's grace, accepting God's pardon, and together striving to help free each other from bonds of fear, despair and meaninglessness, fitting for lives in commitment, responsibility, witness, service, and celebration in God's kingdom, we will share in this venture as children of God and brothers and sisters in Christ toward wholeness.

United Presbyterian Church in the USA: 182nd General Assembly. The 182nd General Assembly expresses special interest in and support of research projects concerning homosexuality. It calls on the churches to support and give leadership in movements toward the elimination of laws governing the private sexual behavior of consenting adults.

188th General Assembly

I.   THE ALL-ENCOMPASSING GRACE OF GOD

We affirm once again that every person, without limitation, is the object of God's gracious love in Jesus Christ. Only by approaching the subject of homosexuality with love, compassion, prayer and honesty, can our Church continue in its great Reformed tradition.

II.   GOD CONTINUES TO REVEAL HIS WILL

Because God continues to reveal more of himself and his will in each succeeding age, we do not believe that a position in any one period sets forth the final understanding of his word to the Church. We know that there is always more light to break forth from the Bible through the work of the Holy Spirit. Jesus said, "I have many things to say to you, but you cannot hear them now. When the Spirit of Truth comes, he will guide you into all the truth." (John 16:12–13)

III. WE MUST DECLARE OUR PRESENT UNDERSTANDING.

Nevertheless, in the life of the Church today, it is necessary, as in ages past, to declare a present understanding of God's will for the guidance of his people in the real issues they face.

IV. REQUEST FOR GUIDANCE CONCERNING HOMOSEXUALITY

The issue of homosexuality in general, and the specific issue of ordination of avowed practicing homosexuals, has been presented to us in several overtures. This raises new and perplexing problems for our Church. We recognize that many expressions of homosexuality are without question sinful in the eyes of God. We are cautious in our judgment, at this time in the history of our Church, because a person who is an avowed homosexual but who is otherwise well qualified has asked to be ordained to the professional ministry of the Gospel. A committee of his presbytery finds nothing in his life or witness in any way questionable on Christian grounds except the one issue of his alternate sexual orientation. And though we reaffirm the right of the presbytery to take what action it seems best, consistent with the Book of Order, we are rightly called to give guidance to the presbytery as it faces its decision.

V. OUR CHURCH's CURRENT POSITION

Therefore, the 188th General Assembly calls to the attention of our Church that, according to our most recent statement we "reaffirm our adherence to the moral law of God . . . that . . . the practice of homosexuality is sin . . . Also we affirm that any self-righteous attitude of others who would condemn persons who have so sinned is also sin." (GA Minutes of 1970, Part I, p. 469). The 188th General Assembly declares again its commitment to this statement. Therefore, on broad Scriptural and confessional grounds, it appears that it would at the present time be injudicious, if not improper, for a presbytery to ordain to the professional ministry of the Gospel a person who is an avowed practicing homosexual.

VI. WE NEED TO SEEK MORE LIGHT

However, humbly remembering the way past General Assembly positions sometimes have changed as further light has been given, the 188th General Assembly directs that a task force be established, related to the Advisory Council on Church and Society, to study these issues. Members of the task force shall be appointed by the Moderator of the 188th General Assembly acting in concert with the Chairperson of the Church and Society Advisory Council. The task force shall include a preponderance of people broadly representative of the life of our Church, both ministers and laypersons. It is expected that the task force shall include or consult with experts in such fields as biblical interpretation, theology, ethics, psychology, sociology and law. It is furthermore expected that the task force shall be expected to circulate to the churches materials designed to discover attitudes within our Church on the subject and to provide information back to the church. The work of the task force shall be reported annually to the General Assembly.

VIII. THE UNITY OF THE CHURCH IN FAITHFULNESS TO CHRIST

The 188th General Assembly moreover declares its profound intention, as this issue is discussed, to preserve under the Lordship of Jesus Christ both the unity of the Church and our faithfulness to the Bible. We move ahead believing that all truth, known and unknown, is hidden in Jesus Christ, who said of the Spirit who leads us on, "He will glorify me. . ." (John 16:14a). Let us remember the words of I John 4:7, 8: "Beloved, let us love one another, for love is of God, and he who loves is born of God and knows God. He who does not love does not know God: for God is love."

United Church of Christ: Part of Resolution of its Council for Christian Social Action, April 12, 1969.

Whereas homosexual practices between consenting adults in private endanger none of the properly protective functions of civil law, and

Whereas laws against consential [*sic*] homosexual practices between adults in private violate the right of privacy and are virtually unenforceable, except through the abhorent [*sic*] practice of police entrapment and enticement, and

Whereas such laws have no effect on the degree of homosexuality (as indicated by various studies abroad showing that homosexuality exists to no greater extent in countries without such laws than in the United States), and

Whereas present laws and government practices regarding employment and military service of homosexuals are based on false assumptions about the nature of homosexuality in general and the danger of homosexuals to society in particular,

Therefore, the Council for Christian Social Action hereby declares its opposition to all laws which make private homosexual relations between consenting adults a crime and thus urges their repeal. The CCSA also expresses its opposition to the total exclusion of homosexuals from public employment and from enlistment and induction into the armed forces, especially the dismissal with less than honorable discharges from the armed forces for those involved in homosexual practices with consenting adults in private.

Finally, the CCSA encourages the UCC conferences, associations and local churches to hold seminars, consultations, conferences, etc. for honest and open discussion of the nature of homosexuality in our society.

United Methodist Church: Part of the Social Principles of the United Methodist Church adopted by the 1972 General Conference:

Homosexuals no less than heterosexuals are persons of sacred worth who need the ministry and guidance of the Church in their struggles for human fulfillment, as well as the spiritual and emotional care of a fellowship which enables reconciling relationships with God, wih [*sic*] others and with self. Further we must insist that all persons are entitled to have their human and civil rights insured, though we do not condone the practice of homosexuality and consider this practice incompatible with Christian teaching.

THE CHURCH
AND
HOMOSEXUALITY,
1978

*The United Presbyterian Church
in the United States of America*

Preface

The 188th General Assembly (1976) of The United Presbyterian Church in the United States of America directed "that a task force be established, related to its Advisory Council on Church and Society," to study "Christian approaches to homosexuality, with special reference to the ordination of avowed practicing homosexuals." The work of the task force was to be reported annually to the General Assembly.

The task force was appointed, at the direction of the General Assembly, jointly by the Moderator of the 188th General Assembly (1976), Dr. Thelma C. D. Adair, and the then Chairperson of the Advisory Council on Church and Society, Ms. Jeanne C. Marshall. It was further directed that the task force be composed of "people broadly representative of the life of our church, both ministers and laypersons . . . experts in such fields as biblical interpretation, theology, ethics, psychiatry, sociology, and law" and that those persons "shall represent a spectrum of all sides of these issues."

Appointment of the full task force was announced by Dr. Adair and Ms. Marshall on September 24, 1976. The nineteen members were:

Ms. Virginia West Davidson, Rochester, NY, Chairperson

Rev. Wilbur R. Brandli, White Pigeon, MI

Rev. Gail G. Buchwalter, Pittsburgh, PA

Rev. Donald Reed Caughey, Ellensburg, WA

Rev. Robert M. Davidson, New York, NY

Dr. John Duckett, Philadelphia, PA

Rev. George R. Edwards, Louisville, KY (on sabbatical leave in West Germany beginning June 1977)

Mr. Chris Glaser, West Hollywood, CA

Dr. Willard Heckel, Newark, NJ

Rev. Virgil L. Jones, Detroit, MI

Rev. Richard Lovelace, Hamilton, MA

Rev. Aahmes E. Overton, Hayward, CA

Rev. Byron E. Shafer, Yonkers, NY

Rev. Robert E. Simpson, St. Louis, MO

Mr. Dwight C. Smith, Jr., Loudonville, NY

Rev. Gloria Tate, Indianapolis, IN

Rev. Kenneth L. Vaux, Houston, TX

Ms. Barbara P. White, Cleveland Heights, OH

Rev. Donald M. Williams, Van Nuys, CA.

Task force members encompassed a broad range of theological perspectives and experience, and a number were specialists in fields related to the task force's area of study.

The task force met seven times: October 14–16, 1976, in Chicago; December 2–4, 1976, in St. Louis; February 17–19, 1977, in Houston; June 22 and 25, 1977, in Philadelphia; August 24–27, 1977, in Chicago; October 14–16, 1977, in St. Louis; and January 4–7, 1978, in New York City. Presentations were given by task force members and other experts on the major biblical, theological, historical, ethical, biomedical, and psychological issues. The task force also met with Dr. Adair and Ms. Marshall.

Regional hearings were held in order for the task force to hear the church at large: March 10–12, 1977, in Cleveland; March 31–April 2, 1977, in St. Louis; May 19–21, 1977, in San Francisco; June 23–24, 1977, in Philadelphia, in conjunction with the meeting of the 189th General Assembly (1977).

Other ways in which the task force learned the church's present attitudes included a letter to executive presbyters and stated clerks of presbyteries, requesting information about studies taking place within their areas or conclusions already reached; the use of the January 1977 Presbyterian Panel to learn about current attitudes; requests for written personal testimony from those who could not attend a regional hearing and yet wanted to be heard and from persons who have experience as or with homosexual persons, former homosexuals, and others who wanted to inform the task force; and attendance by several task force members at the Consultation on Homosexuality sponsored by Presbyterians United for Biblical Concerns, January 25–27, 1977, in Pittsburgh. In addition, as task force members responded to requests to address presbyteries and other groups, they had opportunity to listen to many Presbyterians' concerns.

Charged by the General Assembly "to circulate to the churches materials designed to discover attitudes within our church on the subject, and to provide information back to the church," the task force prepared two packets of informational and educational materials, which were offered widely for purchase by those who wanted to engage in a study parallel to the task force's own study. The packets include an annotated bibliography created by the task force, transcripts from some of the task force meetings, papers prepared by task force members, and other papers on specific technical subjects. More than 6,000 packets have been ordered since they first became available in April 1977.

In its prospectus for study prepared by the Advisory Council on Church and Society and accepted by the task force at its first meeting, the group's purpose was described this way:

1. Identify and evaluate various theological and biblical perspectives on homosexuality, giving attention to specific biblical texts and themes. Give attention to confessional stands and specific attention to the positions taken by the 182nd General Assembly (1970).

2. Survey general studies and research, and assess theories and assumptions about homosexuality in light of biblical and theological perspectives and current understandings about homosexuality in the social and behavioral sciences, in homophile groups, and in society at large.

3. Identify and evaluate areas of ethical concern, with particular emphasis on personal freedom, personal responsibility, and human rights, and discriminatory practices, both in the church and in society generally.

4. Suggest guidelines for faithful Christian response to the conflicts between values, rights, and human communities manifest in relation to homosexuality, both in the life of the church, including ordination, and with respect to broad social policies.

The task force completed its work and on January 12, 1978, transmitted to the Advisory Council on Church and Society a background paper, policy statement, and recommendations, and a minority policy statement and recommendations. The chairperson of the task force observed in transmitting the report:

> During the months of study, reading, listening, and writing, we have at times tested the possible limits of diversity beyond which we would not continue to exist as a task force. We never exceeded those limits, I believe, because we remained faithful in our intent to listen to one another carefully and seriously challenge each other; to respect one another's opinions and insights; to try honestly to stand in each other's shoes and thus discover how it might feel for someone else. At times we either argued or agreed with one another; laughed or cried with each other; shared our deepest burdens or joys with one another; listened carefully or confronted each other, forgave and loved each other; played, prayed, and sang with each other; and broke bread together around our Lord's table.
>
> We transmit all of these documents to you as evidence of how far we have come together on this journey, and how far we still have to go. Where we agree, perhaps it will be seen as a small sign of the inbreaking of God's kingdom in our midst. Taken together, the documents represent our rich diversities within the unity we have in Christ as a part of his body. It is to Christ we are all bound; and it is as we gather around his table, humbly and with thanksgiving, that we are made whole.

On January 16, 1978, the Advisory Council on Church and Society voted to transmit the report and its recommendations, together with the minority statement and recommendations, to the General Assembly for decision. The Advisory Council recommended that the General Assembly adopt the statement and recommendations proposed by the majority of the task force, with three members recording their negative votes.

Following regular United Presbyterian procedures, the full report was printed immediately and circulated to all those persons elected by the presbyteries as commissioners to the 190th General Assembly (1978), called to convene on May 16, 1978, in San Diego, California. Extra copies were printed and 20,540 were purchased by individuals and church groups for further intensive study.

According to the rules of the General Assembly, the report was placed in the hands of a committee composed of forty-four commissioners elected by the General Assembly and a chairperson appointed by the newly-elected Moderator. That committee also was given seventeen overtures and twenty-two resolutions from presbyteries related to the issues of homosexuality and a large volume of communications from United Presbyterian congregations and individual members.

The Assembly Committee on the Church and Homosexuality met in plenary session for open hearings and for general discussion of the report submitted to them. A drafting subcommittee then worked in closed session to produce the draft statement and recommendations that were debated and amended by the full assembly committee in an open plenary session. The product of this four-day process was then printed and distributed to all General Assembly commissioners as the document to be debated by the full General Assembly.

On Monday, May 22, 1978, the 190th General Assembly (1978) devoted approximately ten hours to plenary debate and approved the report as printed here. The Office of the General Assembly was directed to print both the background paper, which was received by the General Assembly as a resource for continuing study, and the policy statement and recommendations, which were adopted as the official position of the General Assembly. The Office of the General Assembly was also directed to make copies available to all United Presbyterian congregations and judicatories and to others who wished to order them.

Since persons who are not United Presbyterians may be reading this report, a brief word of explanation as to the status of its contents may be helpful:

1. The background paper "The Church and Homosexuality," by the Reverend Byron E. Shafer, was received by the 190th General Assembly (1978) exactly as submitted to it by the Advisory Council on Church and Society. It is reprinted as an aid to study and does not have official policy status.

2. Sections of the background paper refer to "majority" and "minority" positions within the Task Force to Study Homosexuality. These positions formed the basis of separate recommended policy statements and recommendations that

accompanied the background paper as it was submitted to the General Assembly but which are not printed here since the General Assembly did not approve either as submitted. Readers should understand that "majority" and "minority" positions as reported here reflect the thinking only of the members of the task force and not that of the United Presbyterian membership.

3. The "Statement and Recommendations" printed here are those developed and approved by the 190th General Assembly (1978) itself. They are different from either the "majority" or "minority" reports recommended by the task force, although elements of both are incorporated. As noted, these are the official positions of the General Assembly of the United Presbyterian Church concerning homosexuality.

William P. Thompson
Stated Clerk

New York, New York
June, 1978

Policy Statement and Recommendations

Introduction

The General Assembly was asked by the Presbyteries of New York City and of the Palisades to give "definitive guidance" concerning the eligibility for ordination to the professional ministry of persons who openly acknowledge homosexual orientation and practice. One thing has become very clear in consideration of this request. The church must respond to this issue. Numbers of persons both within the church and outside it experience homosexuality, either as a transient part of their growth as persons or as a continuing force in their own lives or in the lives of family members and friends. New data in psychology and the social sciences have appeared that challenge the church's traditional posture on this matter. The time has come for the church to confront this issue, to reexamine and refresh its theological understanding of homosexuality in the light of God's revelation to us in Jesus Christ, and to renew its practical approach to mission and ministry among homosexual persons.

The issue submitted to this General Assembly is a call for guidance to individual Christian persons, congregations, and presbyteries concerning the status of self-affirming, practicing homosexual persons within the church. Specifically, the presbyteries seek guidance on the matter of ordination to the ministry of Word and Sacrament. Difficult questions are involved in this request. Should the General Assembly foster the creation of a new situation in the church, in which practicing homosexual persons would be free to affirm their lifestyle publicly and to obtain the church's blessing upon this through ordination? Or should the church reaffirm its historic opposition to homosexual behavior? These questions must be dealt with in the context of the whole life and mission of the church. To answer them, we must examine the nature of homosexuality according to current scientific understandings, interpreted within the context of our theological understandings of God's purpose for human life. To this purpose, in all its rich variety, the Scripture attests. Church membership, ordination, pluralism and unity in the church, and the Christian response in ministry and mission must then, in turn, be examined.

Homosexuality Within a Theological Context

New data and hypotheses in psychology, sociology, endocrinology, and the other secular disciplines cannot in themselves determine a shift in the church's posture on this issue. Very frequently these disciplines shed new light upon our understanding of homosexuality and how the church should respond to it. Frequently the results of scientific inquiry are tentative and inconclusive, neutral in their theological and ethical implications, or even weighted with unspoken values and assumptions that are misleading against the background of biblical faith. Therefore, we must address the task of theologically interpreting these extrabiblical data, while at the same time renewing our understanding of Scripture and tradition in the light of those data in the sciences.

Medical and psychological theories concerning homosexuality and its causes are complex and often contradictory. Among the multitude of hypotheses and conclusions currently being entertained, a small but significant body of facts emerges that enlarges our understanding of what homosexuality is and how we should respond to it. It seems clear that homosexuality is primarily a matter of affectional attraction that cannot be defined simply in terms of genital acts, although the homosexual orientation may be so expressed.

Most human beings experience occasional homosexual attraction, although not always consciously. It is reasonably certain that somewhere between 5 and 10 percent of the human population is exclusively or predominantly homosexual in orientation. Exclusively homosexual persons appear to be remarkably resistant to reorientation through most psychiatric methods. Most exclusively homosexual persons believe that their condition is irreversible. Some secular therapists working with those motivated to change report some success in reversal, and counselors employing both the resources of Christian faith and psychotherapeutic techniques report a higher rate of success. It appears that two critical variables are involved. First, do therapist and client believe that change is possible? Second, how convinced is the client that change is desirable?

The causes of homosexuality now appear to be remarkably numerous and diverse. There is no one explanation for homosexual affectional preference, and thus neither the persons involved nor their parents can be singled out as responsible for the homosexual orientation. Most authorities now assume that both heterosexuality and homosexuality result primarily from psychological and social factors affecting human beings during their growth toward maturity, with some possible influence from biological factors. Most homosexual persons do not consciously choose their affectional preference, although they do face the choice of whether to accept it or to seek change, and of whether to express it in genital acts or to remain celibate. However, although homosexual affectional preference is not always the result of conscious choice, it may be interpreted as part of the involuntary and often unconscious drive away from God's purposes that characterizes fallen human nature, falling short of God's intended patterns for human sexuality.

Human sexuality has a dynamic quality. Within the constraints of nature, nurture serves to transform both sexual identity and intersexual preference. Our sexuality is vulnerable to shaping influences from many directions.

As the embryo develops, the single root organism unfolds and differentiates, sometimes making a boy, sometimes a girl, sometimes a sexually ambiguous being. Following an initial gender assignment, we believe and nurture ourselves and one another into authentic or inauthentic sexual beings.

We find here a parallel to the Genesis account of the creation of humankind, which speaks of the precious and precarious balance of male and female life together that perpetually needs both our affirmation and God's upholding grace. Genesis offers polemic against deviations from the wise separation of humankind into man and woman. It is this separation that makes union possible. In creation, God separates woman from man so that they are constituted with yearning for each other. Becoming one flesh they portray the glory of his image in the earth.

To say that God created humankind male and female, called man and woman to join in partnership as one flesh, and commanded them to multiply (Genesis 1:27–28; 2:24) is to describe how God intended loving companionship between a man and a woman to be a fundamental pattern of human relationship and the appropriate context for male-female genital sexual expression. However, to say that God created humankind male and female, called man and woman to join in partnership as one flesh, and commanded them to multiply is not to state that God intended to limit the possibility for meaningful life to heterosexual marriage. Jesus' own celibate lifestyle and his commitment to his own ministry rather than to the biological family (Matthew 12:46–50; Mark 3:31–35; Luke 8:19–21) demonstrates the blessing of God upon life lived outside the covenant of marriage.

This biological and theological argument has implications for homosexuality. It appears that one explanation of the process in which persons develop homosexual preferences and behavior is that men and women fall away from their intended being because of distorted or insufficient belief in who they are. They are not adequately upheld in being male and female, in being heterosexual, by self-belief and the belief of a supporting community.

Therefore, it appears that what is really important is not what homosexuality is but what we believe about it. Our understanding of its nature and causes is inconclusive, medically and psychologically. Our beliefs about homosexuality thus become paramount in importance. Do we value it, disvalue it, or find it morally neutral? Do we shape an environment that encourages movement toward homosexuality or one that nurtures heterosexual becoming?

We conclude that homosexuality is not God's wish for humanity. This we affirm, despite the fact that some of its forms may be deeply rooted in an individual's personality structure. Some persons are exclusively homosexual in orientation. In many cases homosexuality is more a sign of the brokenness of God's world than of willful rebellion. In other cases homosexual behavior is freely chosen or learned in environments where normal development is thwarted. Even where the homosexual orientation has not been consciously sought or chosen, it is neither a gift from God nor a state nor a condition like race; it is a result of our living in a fallen world.

How are we to find the light and freedom promised to us by our Lord through the Holy Spirit in such a world? Where do we find norms for authentic life, which in truth transcend the conditioning of history and culture, and the power to live by them?

We dare begin no other place than with the living Word, Jesus Christ, who in risen power transcends time and space and the limitations of our values, norms, and assumptions to confront, judge, and redeem us. It is here that all theological confession and affirmation must begin—in the light of God as revealed to us in the incarnate and living Word, Jesus Christ. It is his exposure of our sin, his obedient sacrificial love, and his being raised in power to continue his activity of redemption of this world (I Cor. 15:20–28) that brings us new light. This same God in Jesus Christ comes to make us whole, to redeem creation, and to restore it to the goodness proclaimed at creation. Yet the prelude to this redemption is divine judgment.

To look at the Christ is to see at once the brokenness of the world in which we live and the brokenness of our own lives. This comes as the supreme crisis in our life.

Yet, in the moment of this crisis, the Spirit of God brings the confirmation of divine forgiveness, moves us to respond in faith, repentance, and obedience, and initiates the new life in Christ.

Jesus Christ calls us out of the alienation and isolation of our fallen state into the freedom of new life. This new life redeems us as sexual beings but is impossible without repentance. To claim that God's love for us removes divine judgment of us is to eliminate the essence of divine love and to exchange grace for romantic sentimentality. There is a necessary judgment in God's love—else it cannot redeem. It was this Christ who said to the woman in adultery, "Go and sin no more" (John 8:1–12), and to the rich young ruler: "One thing you still lack.

Sell all that you have and distribute to the poor . . . and come, follow me." (Luke 18:22 and parallels.)

Jesus Christ calls us out of the alienation, brokenness, and isolation of our fallen state into the freedom of new life in Christ. We deny that this new life liberates us to license and affirm that it frees and empowers us for lives of obedience whereby all of life becomes subject to his Lordship.

Scripture and Homosexuality

We have already indicated that we must examine scientific data but must move beyond them in order to understand what our sexuality means and how it should be expressed. We anchor our understanding of homosexuality in the revelation in Scripture of God's intention for human sexuality.

In order to comprehend the biblical view of homosexuality, we cannot simply limit ourselves to those texts that directly address this issue. We must first understand something of what the Scriptures teach about human sexuality in general. As we examine the whole framework of teaching bearing upon our sexuality from Genesis onward, we find that homosexuality is a contradiction of God's wise and beautiful pattern for human sexual relationships revealed in Scripture and affirmed in God's ongoing will for our life in the Spirit of Christ. It is a confusion of sexual roles that mirrors the tragic inversion in which men and women worship the creature instead of the Creator. God created us male and female to display in clear diversity and balance the range of qualities in God's own nature. The opening chapters of Genesis show that sexual union as "one flesh" is established within the context of companionship and the formation of the family. Nature confirms revelation in the functional compatibility of male and female genitalia and the natural process of procreation and family continuity.

Human sin has deeply affected the processes by which sexual orientation is formed, with the result that none of us, heterosexual or homosexual, fulfill perfectly God's plan for our sexuality. This makes it all the more imperative for revelation to make clear for us how our sexual relationships are to be conducted so as to please God and challenge us to seek God's will instead of following our own. Though none of us will ever achieve perfect fulfillment of God's will, all Christians are responsible to view their sins as God views them and to strive against them. To evade this responsibility is to permit the church to model for the world forms of sexual behavior that may seriously injure individuals, families, and the whole fabric of human society. Homosexual persons who will strive toward God's revealed will in this area of their lives, and make use of all the resources of grace, can receive God's power to transform their desires or arrest their active expression.

Within the context of general biblical teaching on human sexuality, a number of passages dealing specifically with homosexuality are significant for our response to this issue. These are, of course, complementary to the wider biblical themes of creation, fall, and redemption.

Three Scriptures specifically address the issue of homosexual behavior between consenting males: Leviticus 18:22, Leviticus 20:13, and Romans 1:26–27. Romans 1:26–27 also addresses the issue of homosexual behavior between consenting females. These three passages stand in an integral and complementary relationship. Leviticus 20:13 regards homosexual behavior as an "abomination."

In the Reformed tradition, the Leviticus passages are considered part of the moral law and thus are different in kind from Levitical proscriptions against certain foods, for instance, which belong to the ritual law. Jesus declared "all foods clean" (Mark 7:19)—one declaration among many that the ritual law of the Old Testament is transcended and fulfilled in him. Moral law in the New Testament is not the means of salvation, for that is Christ alone. Rather, obedience to the moral law is a fruit of grace and salvation.

Genesis 19:1–29 and Judges 19:16–26 show that homosexual rape is a violation of God's justice. II Peter 2:6–10 and Jude 7 suggest a wider context of homosexual practice in Sodom, implying that such rape was but one expression of prior homosexual practice in the population.

Romans 1:26–27 speaks to the problem of homosexual passion, describing it as "dishonorable," as well as to homosexual behavior, which is described as "unnatural." By "unnatural" the Scripture does not mean contrary to custom, nor contrary to the preference of a particular person, but rather contrary to that order of universal human sexual nature that God intended in Genesis 1 and 2.

We emphasize that Paul here includes homosexual behavior in a larger catalog of sins, which includes pride, greed, jealousy, disobedience to parents, and deceit. Homosexual behavior is no greater a sin and no less a sin than these.

Two other texts, I Corinthians 6:9–10 and I Timothy 1:9–10, show further New Testament opposition to homosexual behavior. I Corinthians probably distinguishes between the more passive partners or catamites (*malakoí*) and the more active partners (*arsenokoítai*). Homosexual relationships in the Hellenistic world were widespread. We may safely assume that some were characterized by tenderness, commitment, and altruism. Yet the New Testament declares that all homosexual practice is incompatible with Christian faith and life. No Scriptures speak of homosexuality as granted by God. No Scriptures permit or condone any of the forms of homosexuality. In Matthew 19:1–12, Jesus reaffirms God's intention for sexual intercourse, enduring marriage between husband and wife, and affirms godly celibacy for those not entering the marriage covenant.

The biblical revelation to Israel, reaffirmed in the teaching of Jesus and Paul, portrayed in the *theology and human creation,* specifically reflected in the ethical teaching in both the Old and New Testaments, and confirmed in nature, clearly indicates that genital sexual expression is meant to occur within the covenant of heterosexual marriage. Behavior that is pleasing to God cannot simply be defined as that which pleases others or expresses our own strong needs and identity; it must flow out of faithful and loving obedience to God. Sin cannot simply be defined as behavior that is selfish or lustful. Many unselfish deeds ignore God's expressed intentions for our lives. Homosexual Christians who fail to recognize God's revealed intent for sexual behavior and who move outside God's will in this area of their lives may show many gifts and graces. They may evidence more grace than heterosexual believers who so readily stand in judgment over them. This does not mean that God approves their behavior in the area in which they are failing to be obedient.

To conclude that the Spirit contradicts in our experience what the Spirit clearly said in Scripture is to set Spirit against Spirit and to cut ourselves loose from any objective test to confirm that we are following God and not the spirits in our culture or our own fallible reason. The church that destroys the balance between Word and Spirit, so carefully constructed by the Reformers to insure that we follow none other than Jesus Christ who is the Word, will soon lose its Christian substance and become indistinguishable from the world. We have been charged to seek "new light from God's Word," not "new light" contrary to God's Word.

Church Membership

Persons who manifest homosexual behavior must be treated with the profound respect and pastoral tenderness due all people of God. There can be no place within the Christian faith for the response to homosexual persons of mingled contempt, hatred, and fear that is called homophobia.

Homosexual persons are encompassed by the searching love of Christ. The church must turn from its fear and hatred to move toward the homosexual community in love and to welcome homosexual inquirers to its congregations. It should free them to be candid about their identity and convictions, and it should also share honestly and humbly with them in seeking the vision of God's intention for the sexual dimensions of their lives.

As persons repent and believe, they become members of Christ's body. The church is not a citadel of the morally perfect; it is a hospital for sinners. It is the fellowship where contrite, needy people rest their hope for salvation on Christ and his righteousness. Here in community they seek and receive forgiveness and new life. The church must become the nurturing community so that all whose lives come short of the glory of God are converted, reoriented, and built up into Christian maturity. It may be only in the context of loving community, appreciation, pastoral care, forgiveness, and nurture that homosexual persons can come to a clear understanding of God's pattern for their sexual expression.

There is room in the church for all who give honest affirmation to the vows required for membership in the church. Homosexual persons who sincerely affirm

"Jesus Christ is my Lord and Savior" and "I intend to be his disciple, to obey his word, and to show his love" should not be excluded from membership.

Ordination

To be an ordained officer is to be a human instrument, touched by divine powers but still an earthen vessel. As portrayed in Scripture, the officers set before the church and community an example of piety, love, service, and moral integrity. Officers are not free from repeated expressions of sin. Neither are members and officers free to adopt a lifestyle of conscious, continuing, and unresisted sin in any area of their lives. For the church to ordain a self-affirming, practicing homosexual person to ministry would be to act in contradiction to its charter and calling in Scripture, setting in motion both within the church and society serious contradictions to the will of Christ.

The repentant homosexual person who finds the power of Christ redirecting his or her sexual desires toward a married heterosexual commitment, or finds God's power to control his or her desires and to adopt a celibate lifestyle, can certainly be ordained, all other qualifications being met. Indeed, such candidates must be welcomed and be free to share their full identity. Their experience of hatred and rejection may have given them a unique capacity for love and sensitivity as wounded healers among heterosexual Christians, and they may be incomparably equipped to extend the church's outreach to the homosexual community.

We believe that Jesus Christ intends the ordination of officers to be a sign of hope to the church and the world. Therefore our present understanding of God's will precludes the ordination of persons who do not repent of homosexual practice.

Pluralism and Unity in the Church

We of the 190th General Assembly (1978) realize that not all United Presbyterians can in conscience agree with our conclusions. Some are persuaded that there are forms of homosexual behavior that are not sinful and that persons who practice these forms can legitimately be ordained.

This is wholly in keeping with the diversity of theological viewpoint and the pluralism of opinion that characterize the United Presbyterian Church. We are concerned not to stifle these diverging opinions and to encourage those who hold them to remain within the church. As Paul clearly teaches in Eph. 4:1–16, as members of Christ's body we desperately need one another. None of us is perfect. No opinion or decision is irreformable. Nor do we mean to close further study of homosexuality among the presbyteries and congregations. Quite the contrary, the action we recommend to the judicatories includes a firm direction to study this matter further, so that fear and hatred of homosexual persons may be healed and mission and ministry to homosexual persons strengthened and increased. The pluralism that can bring paralyzing weakness to the church when groups pursue their vision in isolation from one another can bring health and vigor when they practice pluralism-in-dialogue.

We want this dialogue to continue. Nevertheless, we judge that it cannot effectively be pursued in the uncertainty and insecurity that would be generated by the Assembly's silence on this matter at this time. On the basis of our understanding that the practice of homosexuality is sin, we are concerned that homosexual believers and the observing world should not be left in doubt about the church's mind on this issue during any further period of study. Even some who see some forms of homosexual behavior as moral are concerned that persons inside and outside the church will stumble in their faith and understanding if this matter is unresolved.

Ministry and Mission

In ministry the church seeks to express and portray the grace and mercy of Christ in worship, nurture, evangelism, and service to those within the covenant community. In mission the church proclaims to all the good news of redemption and reconciliation, calls persons and nations to repentant faith in Christ, and promotes and demonstrates the advance of his rule in history through healing works of mercy and prophetic witness that aim at justice and liberation.

In its ministry and mission the church must offer both to homosexual persons and to those who fear and hate them God's gracious provision of redemption and forgiveness. It must call both to repentant faith in Christ, urging both toward loving obedience to God's will.

The church's grappling with the issue of homosexuality has already energized its membership in a remarkable awakening of prayer and theological study. Our study should continue with the aim of reaching harmony in our diverging positions on homosexuality and other crucial issues. Our prayer should now be concentrated upon this process of internal reconciliation and also upon the creation of ministry with homosexual persons. Great love and care must be exercised toward homosexual persons already within our church, both those who have affirmed their sexual identity and practice and those who have in conscience chosen not to do so. We urge candidates committees, ministerial relations committees, personnel committees, nominating committees, and judicatories to conduct their examination of candidates for ordained office with discretion and sensitivity, recognizing that it would be a hindrance to God's grace to make a specific inquiry into the sexual orientation or practice of candidates for ordained office or ordained officers where the person involved has not taken the initiative in declaring his or her sexual orientation.

The Christian community can neither condone nor participate in the widespread contempt for homosexual persons that prevails in our general culture. Indeed, beyond this, it must do everything in its power to prevent society from continuing to hate, harass, and oppress them. The failure of the church to demonstrate grace in its life has contributed to the forcing of homosexual persons into isolated communities. This failure has served to reinforce the homosexual way of life and to heighten alienation from both church and society. The church should be a spiritual and moral vanguard leading society in response to homosexual persons.

Through direct challenge and support the church should encourage the public media—television, film, the arts, and literature—to portray in a wholesome manner robust, fully human life expressing the finer qualities of the human spirit. It should call upon its members and agencies to work to eliminate prejudicial and stereotypical images of homosexual persons in the public media.

Decriminalization and Civil Rights

There is no legal, social, or moral justification for denying homosexual persons access to the basic requirements of human social existence. Society does have a legitimate role in regulating some sexual conduct, for criminal law properly functions to preserve public order and decency and to protect citizens from public offense, personal injury, and exploitation. Thus, criminal law properly prohibits homosexual and heterosexual acts that involve rape, coercion, corruption of minors, mercenary exploitation, or public display. However, homosexual and heterosexual acts in private between consenting adults involve none of these legitimate interests of society. Sexual conduct in private between consenting adults is a matter of private morality to be instructed by religious precept or ethical example and persuasion, rather than by legal coercion.

Vigilance must be exercised to oppose federal, state, and local legislation that discriminates against persons on the basis of sexual orientation and to initiate and support federal, state, or local legislation that prohibits discrimination against persons on the basis of sexual orientation in employment, housing, and public accommodations. This provision would not affect the church's employment policies.

Conclusions

I. Response to Overture 9 (1976)

The Presbytery of New York City and the Presbytery of the Palisades have asked the General Assembly to give "definitive guidance" in regard to the ordination of persons who may be otherwise well qualified but who affirm their own homosexual identity and practice.

The phrase "homosexual persons" does not occur in the Book of Order of the United Presbyterian Church. No phrase within the Book of Order explicitly prohibits the ordination of self-affirming, practicing homosexual persons to office within the church. However, no phrase within the Book of Order can be construed as an explicit mandate to disregard sexual practice when evaluating candidates for ordination. In short, the Book of Order does not give explicit direction to presbyteries, elders, and congregations as to whether or not self-affirming, practicing homosexual persons are eligible or ineligible for ordination to office.

Therefore, the 190th General Assembly (1978) of The United Presbyterian Church in the United States of America offers the presbyteries the following definitive guidance:

That unrepentant homosexual practice does not accord with the requirements for ordination set forth in Form of Government, Chapter VII, Section 3 (37.03): . . . "It is indispensable that, besides possessing the necessary gifts and abilities, natural and acquired, everyone undertaking a particular ministry should have a sense of inner persuasion, be sound in the faith, live according to godliness, have the approval of God's people and the concurring judgment of a lawful judicatory of the Church."

In relation to candidates for the ordained ministry, committees should be informed by the above guidance.

II. Recommendations

Consistent with this policy statement and conclusions, the 190th General Assembly (1978):

1. Adopts this policy statement and directs the Office of the General Assembly to send a copy of the policy statement to all congregations, presbyteries, and synods and to provide it for widespread distribution.

2. Receives the background paper of the Task Force to Study Homosexuality as a study document, and directs the Office of the General Assembly to provide copies to all congregations, presbyteries, and synods and to make such copies available to others upon request.

3. Urges judicatories, agencies, and local churches to undertake a variety of educational activities, using both formal and informal church structures and organizations.

   a. Since homosexuality is one issue that helps clarify our general responsibility to God in the world and focuses many dimensions of belief and action, such educational activities should probe such basic issues as (1) the strengthening of family life; (2) ministry to single persons and affirmation of their full participation in the Christian community; (3) nurturing lifestyles in our families, congregations, and communities that celebrate the values of friendship with peers of one's own sex and the opposite sex, committed choice of lifemates, joyous and loving fidelity within marriage, the establishment of homes where love and care can nurture strong children able to give loving service to others, and the fashioning of an atmosphere of justice, truth, and kindness that signals Christ's presence; (4) understanding how to extend ministries of deep concern and challenge to those who through choice or circumstance are sexually active, homosexually or heterosexually, outside the covenant of marriage; (5) helping those whose ability to show loving concern is destroyed by homophobia—the irrational fear of and contempt for homosexual persons.

b. Workshops in synods and presbyteries should be conducted both to explore ways to help homosexual persons participate in the life of the church and to discover new ways of reaching out to homosexual persons outside the church.

c. Courses on sexuality should be initiated by seminaries, colleges, and churches to provide officers and members with a systematic understanding of the dynamics of human sexuality as understood within the context of Christian ethics.

d. Contact and dialogue should be encouraged among groups and persons of all persuasions on the issue of homosexuality.

4. Urges presbyteries and congregations to develop outreach programs to communities of homosexual persons beyond the church to allow higher levels of rapport to emerge.

5. Urges agencies of the General Assembly, as appropriate, to develop responses to the following needs:

a. Support for outreach programs by presbyteries and congregations to homosexual persons beyond the church to allow higher levels of rapport to emerge.

b. Encouragement of contact and dialogue among groups and persons who disagree on whether or not homosexuality is sinful per se and whether or not homosexual persons may be ordained as church officers.

c. Development of structures to counsel and support homosexual persons concerned about their sexuality and their Christian faith.

d. Development of pastoral counseling programs for those affected or offended by the decision of this General Assembly.

6. Urges candidates committees, personnel committees, nominating committees, and judicatories to conduct their examination of candidates for ordained office with discretion and sensitivity, recognizing that it would be a hindrance to God's grace to make a specific inquiry into the sexual orientation or practice of candidates for ordained office or ordained officers where the person involved has not taken the initiative in declaring his or her sexual orientation.

7. Calls upon the media to continue to work to end the use of harmful stereotypes of homosexual persons; and encourages agencies of the General Assembly,

presbyteries, and congregations to develop strategies to insure the end of such abuse.

8. Calls on United Presbyterians to reject in their own lives, and challenge in others, the sin of homophobia, which drives homosexual persons away from Christ and his church.

9. Encourages persons working in the human sciences and therapies to pursue research that will seek to learn more about the nature and causes of homosexuality.

10. Encourages the development of support communities of homosexual Christians seeking sexual reorientation or meaningful, joyous, and productive celibate lifestyles and the dissemination throughout the church of information about such communities.

11. Encourages seminaries to apply the same standards for homosexual and heterosexual persons applying for admission.

12. Reaffirms the need, as expressed by the 182nd General Assembly (1970) for United Presbyterians to work for the decriminalization of private homosexual acts between consenting adults, and calls for an end to the discriminatory enforcement of other criminal laws against homosexual persons.

13. Calls upon United Presbyterians to work for the passage of laws that prohibit discrimination in the areas of employment, housing, and public accommodations based on the sexual orientation of a person.

14. Declares that these actions shall not be used to affect negatively the ordination rights of any United Presbyterian deacon, elder, or minister who has been ordained prior to this date.

Further the 190th General Assembly (1978) calls upon those who in conscience have difficulty accepting the decisions of this General Assembly bearing on homosexuality to express that conscience by continued dialogue within the church.

HOMOSEXUALITY AND THE CHURCH: A POSITION PAPER, 1979

Presbyterian Church in the United States

The Council on Theology and Culture offers this paper on Homosexuality and the Church as its response to the General Assembly's instruction that the Council study the issue and recommend a position concerning it. In the responses to the study paper, the statements of two previous General Assemblies, the overtures referred to the Council, the Policy Paper adopted by The United Presbyterian Church and commended to the Council by the last General Assembly (all reviewed above) the Council had rather clear directions set to guide the formation of its recommendation. In studying the matter since the meeting of the last Assembly we have reached the conclusion that the Policy Statement adopted by the 190th General Assembly of the United Presbyterian Church states a clear position which is well-grounded biblically and theologically, is appropriate in the light of the guidance received by the Council from the members and courts of the Church, and represents the conclusions of the Council itself. With the permission of the Office of the Stated Clerk of the United Presbyterian Church we present the following paper, a version of the Policy Statement of the United Presbyterian Church adapted to make it appropriate for use in this report and in our church.

Homosexuality Within a Theological Context

New data and hypotheses in psychology, sociology, endocrinology, and the other secular disciplines cannot in themselves determine a shift in the church's posture on this issue. Very frequently these disciplines shed new light upon our understanding of homosexuality and how the church should respond to it. Frequently the results of scientific inquiry are tentative and inconclusive, neutral in their theological and ethical implications, or even weighted with unspoken values and assumptions that are misleading against the background of biblical faith. Therefore we must address the task of theologically interpreting these extrabiblical data, while at the same time renewing our understanding of scripture and tradition in the light of those data in the sciences.

Medical and psychological theories concerning homosexuality and its causes are complex and often contradictory. Among the multitude of hypotheses and conclusions currently being entertained, a small but significant body of facts emerges that enlarges our understanding of what homosexuality is and how we should respond to it. It seems clear that homosexuality is primarily a matter of affectional attraction that cannot be defined simply in terms of genital acts, although the homosexual orientation may be so expressed.

Most human beings experience occasional homosexual attraction, although not always consciously. It is widely reported that somewhere between 5 and 10 percent of the human population is predominantly homosexual in orientation. Predominantly homosexual persons appear to be remarkably resistant to reorientation through most psychiatric methods. Most predominantly homosexual persons believe that their condition is irreversible. Some secular therapists working with those motivated to change report some success in reversal, and counselors employing both the resources of Christian faith and psychotherapeutic techniques report a higher rate of success. It appears that two critical variables are involved. First, do therapist and client believe that change is possible? Second, how convinced is the client that change is desirable?

The causes of homosexuality now appear to be remarkably numerous and diverse. There is no one explanation for homosexual affectional preference, and thus neither the persons involved nor their parents can be singled out as responsible for the homosexual orientation. Most authorities now assume that both heterosexuality and homosexuality result primarily from psychological and social factors affecting human beings during their growth toward maturity, with some possible influence from biological factors. Most homosexual persons do not consciously choose their affectional preference, although they do face the choice of whether to accept it or to seek change, and of whether to express it in genital acts or to remain celibate. However, although homosexual affectional preference is not always the result of conscious choice, it may be interpreted as part of the involuntary and often unconscious drive away from God's purposes that characterizes fallen human nature, falling short of God's intended patterns for human sexuality.

Human sexuality has a dynamic quality. Within the constraints of nature, nurture serves to transform both sexual identity and intersexual preference. Our sexuality is vulnerable to shaping influences from many directions.

As the embryo develops, the single root organism unfolds and differentiates, sometimes making a boy, sometimes a girl, sometimes a sexually ambiguous being. Following an initial gender assignment, we believe and nurture ourselves and one another into authentic or inauthentic sexual being.

The Genesis account of the creation of humankind speaks of the precious balance of male and female life together, which perpetually needs both our affirmation and God's upholding grace. It should be heard as warning against deviations from the wise separation of humankind into man and woman. It is this separation that makes union possible. In creation, God separates woman from man so that they are constituted with yearning for each other. Becoming one flesh they portray the glory of his image in the earth.

To say that God created humankind male and female, called man and woman to join in partnership as one flesh, and commanded them to multiply (Genesis 1:27–28, 2:24) is to describe how God intended loving companionship between a man and a woman to be a fundamental pattern of human relationship and the appropriate context for genital sexual expression. However, to say that God created humankind male and female, called man and woman to join in partnership as one flesh, and commanded them to multiply is not to state that God intended to limit the possibility for meaningful life to heterosexual marriage. Jesus' own celibate lifestyle and his commitment to his own ministry rather than to the biological family (Matthew 12:46–50, Mark 3:31–35, Luke 8:19–21) demonstrates the blessing of God upon life lived outside the covenant of marriage.

This biological and theological argument has implications for homosexuality. It appears that one explanation of the process in which persons develop homosexual preferences and behavior is that men and women fall away from their intended being because of distorted or insufficient belief in who they are. They are not adequately upheld in being male and female, in being heterosexual by self-belief and the belief of a supporting community.

Therefore it appears that what is really important is not what homosexuality is, but what we believe about it. Our understanding of its nature and causes is inconclusive, medically and psychologically. Our beliefs about homosexuality thus become paramount in importance. Do we value it, disvalue it, or find it morally neutral? Do we shape an environment that encourages movement toward homosexuality or one that nurtures heterosexual becoming?

We conclude that homosexuality is not God's wish for humanity. This we affirm, despite the fact that some of its forms may be deeply rooted in an individual's personality structure. Some persons are exclusively homosexual in orientation. In many cases homosexuality is more a sign of the brokenness of God's world than of willful rebellion. In other cases homosexual behavior is freely chosen or learned in environments where normal development is thwarted. Even where the homosexual orientation has not been consciously sought or chosen, it is neither a gift from God nor a state or a condition like race; it is a result of our living in a fallen world.

(The Council on Theology and Culture notes that in this paragraph, and overall, this paper is working with a doctrine of sin which understands it as a feature of human existence which is a much more pervasive and damaging reality than the moral deficiency of a particular act. While the practice of homosexuality is called a sin, the paper does not speak of the homosexual condition as a sin. Rather, to avoid falling into a shallow and moralistic view, it takes the homosexual condition to be an effect of sin whether its origin is thought to be willful, congenital, or social. It is one of those configurations of human character which results from the power of sin in human will, in society and in the world. This understanding of the sinfulness of homosexuality does not preclude the possibility of relatively loving and faithful actions even within the framework of such a condition of sin. Nor should it be viewed as an isolated or even unique manifestation of such sinfulness. Self-righteousness on the part of heterosexual people will be avoided more easily if it is remembered that such human orientations as racism and economic elitism equally manifest the same complex, yet powerful, condition of sinfulness).

How are we to find the light and freedom promised to us by our Lord through the Holy Spirit in a fallen world? Where do we find norms for authentic life which in truth transcend the conditioning of history and culture, and the power to live by them?

We dare begin no other place than with the living Word, Jesus Christ, who in risen power transcends time and space and the limitations of our values, norms, and assumptions, to confront, judge, and redeem us. It is here that all theological confession and affirmation must begin—in the light of God as revealed to us in the incarnate and living Word, Jesus Christ. It is his exposure of our sin, his obedient sacrificial love, and his being raised in power to continue his activity of redemption of this world (I Cor. 15:20–28) that brings us new light. This same God in Jesus Christ comes to make us whole, to redeem creation and to restore it to the goodness proclaimed at creation. It is with a combination of judgment and grace that we are redeemed.

To look at the Christ is to see at once the brokenness of the world in which we live and the brokenness of our own lives. This comes as the supreme crisis in our life.

Yet in the moment of this crisis the Spirit of God brings the confirmation of divine forgiveness, moves us to respond in faith, repentance, and obedience and initiates the new life in Christ.

Jesus Christ calls us out of the alienation and isolation of our fallen state into the freedom of new life. This new life redeems us as sexual beings but is impossible without repentance. To claim that God's love for us removes divine judgment of us is to eliminate the essence of divine love and to exchange grace for romantic sentimentality. There is a necessary judgment in God's love—else it cannot redeem. It was this Christ who said to the woman in adultery "Go and sin no more" (I John 8:1–12) and to the Rich Young Ruler "One thing you still lack. Sell all that you have and distribute to the poor . . . and come, follow me." (Luke 18:22 and parallels.) We deny that this new life liberates us to license and affirm that it frees and empowers us for lives of obedience whereby all life becomes subject to His Lordship.

Scripture and Homosexuality

We have already indicated that we must examine scientific data but must move beyond them in order to understand what our sexuality means and how it should be expressed. We anchor our understanding of homosexuality in the revelation in scripture of God's intention for human sexuality.

In order to comprehend the biblical view of homosexuality, we cannot simply limit ourselves to those texts that directly address this issue. We must first understand something of what the scriptures teach about human sexuality in general. As we examine the whole framework of teaching bearing upon our sexuality from Genesis onward, we find that homosexuality is a contradiction of God's wise and beautiful pattern for human sexual relationships revealed in scripture and affirmed in God's ongoing will for our life in the Spirit of Christ. It is a confusion of sexual roles that mirrors the tragic inversion in which men and women worship the creature instead of the Creator. God created us male and female to display in clear diversity and balance the range of qualities in God's own nature. The opening chapters of Genesis show that sexual union as "one flesh" is established within the context of companionship and the formation of the family. This theological view of human sexuality is coherent with the functional compatibility of male and female genitalia and the natural process of procreation and family continuity.

Human sin has deeply affected the processes by which sexual orientation is formed, with the result that none of us, heterosexual or homosexual, fulfills perfectly God's plan for our sexuality. This makes it all the more imperative for revelation to make clear for us how our sexual relationships are to be conducted so as to please God and challenge us to seek God's will instead of following our own. Though none of us will ever achieve perfect fulfillment of God's will, all Christians are responsible to view their sins as God views them and to strive against them. To evade this responsibility is to permit the church to model for the world forms of sexual behavior that may seriously injure individuals, families, and the whole fabric of human society. Homosexual persons who will strive toward God's revealed will in this area of their lives, and make use of all the resources of grace, can receive God's power to transform their desires or arrest their active expression.

Within the context of general biblical teaching on human sexuality, a number of passages dealing specifically with homosexuality are significant for our response to this issue. These are, of course, complementary to the wider biblical themes of creation, fall and redemption.

Three scriptures specifically address the issue of homosexual behavior between consenting males: Leviticus 18:22, Leviticus 20:13, and Romans 1:26–27. Romans 1:26–27 also addresses the issue of homosexual behavior between consenting females. These three passages stand in an integral and complementary relationship. Leviticus 20:13 regards homosexual behavior as an "abomination."

In the Reformed Tradition, the Leviticus passages are considered a part of the moral law and thus are different in kind from Levitical proscriptions against certain foods, for instance, which belong to the ritual law. Jesus declared "all foods clean" (Mark 7:19), one declaration among many that the ritual law of the Old Testament is transcended and fulfilled in him. Moral law in the New Testament is not the means of salvation, for that is Christ alone. Rather, obedience to the moral law is a fruit of grace and salvation.

Genesis 19:1–29 and Judges 19:16–26 show that homosexual rape is a violation of God's justice. II Peter 2:6–10 and Jude 7 suggest a wider context of homosexual practice in Sodom, implying that such rape was but one expression of prior homosexual practice in the population.

Romans 1:26–27 speaks to the problem of homosexual passion, describing it as "dishonorable," as well as to homosexual behavior, which is described as "unnatural." By "unnatural" the scripture does not mean contrary to custom, nor contrary to the preference of a particular person, but rather contrary to that order of universal human sexual nature that God intended in Genesis 1 and 2.

We emphasize that Paul here includes homosexual behavior in a larger catalogue of sins which includes pride, greed, jealousy, disobedience to parents, and deceit. Homosexual behavior is no greater a sin and no less a sin than these.

Two other texts, I Corinthians 6:9–10 and I Timothy 1:9–10, show further New Testament opposition to homosexual behavior. I Corinthians probably distinguishes between the more passive partners or catamites (malakoi) and the more active partners (arsenokoitai). Homosexual relationships in the Hellinistic [*sic*] World were widespread. We may safely assume that some were characterized by tenderness, commitment, and altruism. Yet the New Testament declares that all homosexual practice is incompatible with Christian faith and life. No scriptures speak of homosexuality as granted by God. No scriptures permit or condone any of the forms of homosexuality. In Matthew 19:1–12, Jesus reaffirms God's intention for sexual intercourse, enduring marriage between husband and wife, and affirms godly celibacy for those not entering the marriage covenant.

The biblical revelation to Israel, reaffirmed in the teaching of Jesus and Paul, portrayed in the theology of human creation, specifically reflected in the ethical teaching in both the Old and New Testaments and confirmed in nature, clearly indicates that genital sexual expression is meant to occur within the covenant of heterosexual marriage. Behavior that is pleasing to God cannot simply be defined as that which pleases others or expresses our own strong needs and identity; it must flow out of faithful and loving obedience to God. Sin cannot simply be defined as behavior that is selfish or lustful. Many unselfish deeds ignore God's expressed intentions for our lives. Homosexual Christians who fail to recognize God's revealed intent for sexual behavior and who move outside God's will in this area of their lives may show many gifts and graces. They may evidence more grace than heterosexual believers who so readily stand in judgment over them. This does not mean that God approves their behavior in the area in which they are failing to be obedient.

To conclude that the Spirit contradicts in our experience what the Spirit has said across the broad range of the canon's testimony is to set Spirit against Spirit and to cut ourselves loose from any objective test to confirm that we are following God and not the spirits in our culture or our own fallible reason. The church that destroys the balance between Word and Spirit, so carefully constructed by the Reformers to insure that we follow none other than Jesus Christ who is the Word, will soon lose its Christian substance and become indistinguishable from the world. We have been charged to seek "new light from God's Word," not "new light" contrary to God's Word.

Church Membership

Persons who manifest homosexual behavior must be treated with the profound respect and pastoral tenderness due all people of God. There can be no place within the Christian faith for the response to homosexual persons of mingled contempt, hatred, and fear that is called homophobia.

As persons repent and believe, they become members of Christ's body. The church is not a citadel of the morally perfect, it is a hospital for sinners. It is the fellowship where contrite, needy people rest their hope for salvation on Christ and his righteousness. Here in community they seek and receive forgiveness and new life. The church must become the nurturing community so that all whose lives come short of the glory of God are converted, reoriented, and built up into Christian maturity. It may be only in the context of loving community, appreciation, pastoral care, forgiveness, and nurture that homosexual persons can come to a clear understanding of God's pattern for their sexual expression.

There is room in the church for all who give honest affirmation to the vows required for membership in the church. Homosexual persons who sincerely make a profession of their faith and obedience should not be excluded from membership.

Ordination

To be an ordained officer is to be a human instrument, touched by divine power but still an earthen vessel. As portrayed in scripture, the officers set before the church and community an example of piety, love, service and moral integrity. Officers are not free from repeated expressions of sin. Neither are members and officers free to adopt a lifestyle of conscious, continuing and unresisted sin in any area of their lives. For the church to ordain a self-affirming practicing homosexual person to ministry would be to act in contradiction to its charter and calling in scripture, setting in motion both within the church and in society serious contradictions to the will of Christ.

The repentant homosexual person who finds the power of Christ redirecting his or her sexual desires toward a married heterosexual commitment, or finds God's power to control his or her desires and to adopt a celibate lifestyle, can certainly be ordained, all other qualifications being met. Indeed, such candidates must be welcomed and be free to share their full identity. Their experience of hatred and rejection may have given them a unique capacity for love and sensitivity as wounded healers among heterosexual Christians, and they may be incomparably equipped to extend the church's outreach to the homosexual community.

We believe that Jesus Christ intends the ordination of officers to be a sign of hope to the church and the world. Therefore our present understanding of God's will precludes the ordination of persons who do not repent of homosexual practice.

Diversity and Unity in the Church

We of the 119th General Assembly (1979) realize that not all members of the Presbyterian Church in the United States can in conscience agree with our conclusions. Some are persuaded that there are forms of homosexual behavior that are not sinful and that persons who practice these forms can legitimately be ordained.

We are concerned not to stifle these diverging opinions and to encourage those who hold them to remain within the church. As Paul clearly teaches in Eph. 4:1–16, as members of Christ's body we desperately need one another. None of us is perfect. No opinion or decision is irreformable. Nor do we mean to close further study of homosexuality among the presbyteries and congregations.

We want dialogue to continue. Nevertheless, we judge that it cannot effectively be pursued in the uncertainty and insecurity that would be generated by the Assembly's silence on this matter at this time. On the basis of our understanding that the practice of homosexuality is sin, we are concerned that homosexual believers and the observing world should not be left in doubt about the church's mind on this issue during any further period and study. Even some who see some forms of homosexual behavior as moral are concerned that persons inside and outside the church will stumble in their faith and understanding if this matter is unresolved.

Ministry and Mission

In ministry the church seeks to express and portray the grace and mercy of Christ in worship, nurture, evangelism, and service to those within the covenant community. In mission the church proclaims to all the good news of redemption and reconciliation, calls persons and nations to repentant faith in Christ, and promotes and demonstrates the advance of his rule in history through healing works of mercy and prophetic witness that aim at justice and liberation.

In its ministry and mission, the church must offer both to homosexual persons and to those who fear and hate them God's gracious provision of redemption and forgiveness. It must call both to repentant faith in Christ, urging both toward loving obedience to God's will.

Great love and care must be exercised toward homosexual persons already within our church, both those who have affirmed their sexual identity and practice and those who have in conscience chosen not to do so. We urge candidate committees, ministerial relations committees, personnel committees, nominating committees, and judicatories to conduct their examination of candidates for ordained office with discretion and sensitivity, recognizing that it would be a hindrance to God's grace to make a specific inquiry into the sexual orientation or practice of candidates for ordained office or ordained officers where the person involved has not taken the initiative in declaring his or her sexual orientation.

The Christian community can neither condone nor participate in the widespread contempt for homosexual persons that prevails in our general culture. Indeed, beyond this, it must do everything in its power to prevent society from continuing to hate, harass, and oppress them. The failure of the church to demonstrate grace in its life has contributed to the forcing of homosexual persons into isolated communities. This failure has served to reinforce the homosexual way of life and to heighten alienation from both church and society. The church should be a spiritual and moral vanguard leading society in response to homosexual persons.

Through direct challenge and support the church should encourage the public media—television, film, the arts and literature—to portray in a wholesome manner robust, fully human life expressing the finer qualities of the human spirit. It should call upon its members and agencies to work to eliminate prejudicial and stereotypical images of homosexual persons in the public media.

Decriminalization and Civil Rights

The 117th and 118th General Assemblies asserted "the need for the church to stand for just treatment of homosexual persons in our society in regard to their civil liberties, equal rights and protection under the law from social and economic discrimination which is due all its citizens." This stand is reaffirmed. It is to be balanced by concern for the civil rights of all those who reject the practice of homosexuality as an acceptable style of life. The church should not be understood as itself encouraging a trend toward demoralization of human sexuality or approving claims of individualism which ignore the involvement of every human being in the society in which life is lived.

[The Standing Committee on Interpreting the Faith recommends]

> 6. That the 119th General Assembly commend this paper and these recommendations to Presbyteries and Sessions as they perform their constitutional duties in the ordination and discipline of Ministers, elders, and deacons (*Book of Church Order* 24–4, 29–1) and in reception and oversight of members (*Book of Church Order,* 15–6).

> 7. That the 119th General Assembly commend this paper along with the study paper, *The Church and Homosexuality: A Preliminary Study,* prepared by the Council on Theology and Culture in 1977, and the study paper, *The Church and Homosexuality,* prepared by the Task Force on Homosexuality of the United Presbyterian Church in 1978, for use in the continuing study of homosexuality and the church.

> 8. That the General Assembly urge all congregations and ministers to continue to develop ministries of compassion and concern with homosexual persons, both

within and without the church, and their families, and to offer counsel and support to homosexual persons concerned about their sexuality in the Christian faith.

9. That the General Assembly urge candidate committees, nominating committees, and judicatories, when dealing with subjects of sexuality and life-style, to conduct their examinations of candidates for ordained office with discretion and sensitivity.

10. That the General Assembly call upon members of the Presbyterian Church in the United States to repent of, in their own lives and to challenge in others, the sins of contempt and hatred toward homosexuals which drive persons away from Christ and his Church.

Rev. John Conner, former Moderator of the UPCUSA, spoke regarding Recommendation 10.

11. That the General Assembly declare that these actions shall not be used to affect negatively the ordination rights of any Deacon, Elder, or Minister who has been ordained prior to this date in the Presbyterian Church in the United States.

(2) That new Recommendation B.12 be added as follows:

12. That the General Assembly instruct the Division of Corporate and Social Mission to establish a Task Force on Homosexuality:

(a) to serve as a nucleus for continuing theological and biblical reflection, study, and dialogue on homosexuality and the church;

(b) to advise the Division of Corporate and Social Mission on directions for resource development; and

(c) to assist the Division in researching existing resources and to develop and make available theological, biblical and educational resources which will aid presbyteries, congregations and ministers in their ministries with homosexual persons and their families. . . .

B. Regarding the Report on the Study of Homosexuality

5. That the General Assembly adopt this paper and direct the Office of the Stated Clerk of the General Assembly to send copies to all ministers and clerks of sessions (see page 361).

6. That the 119th General Assembly commend this paper and these recommendations to presbyteries and sessions as they perform their constitutional duties in the ordination and discipline of ministers (*Book of Church Order* 24–4, 29–1) and in reception and oversight of members (*Book of Church Order* 1–56).

7. That the 119th General Assembly commend this paper along with the study paper, *The Church and Homosexuality: A Preliminary Study,* prepared by the Council on Theology and Culture in 1977, and the study paper, *The Church and*

Homosexuality, prepared by the Task Force on Homosexuality of the United Presbyterian Church in 1978, for use in the continuing study of homosexuality and the church.

8. That the General Assembly urge all congregations and ministers to continue to develop ministries of compassion and concern to homosexual persons and to offer counsel and support to homosexual persons concerned about their sexuality in the Christian faith.

9. That the General Assembly urge candidate committees, nominating committees, and judicatories to conduct their examinations of candidates for ordained office with discretion and sensitivity.

10. That the General Assembly call on members of the Presbyterian Church in the United States to repent of in their own lives, and challenge in others, the sin of homophobia which drives homosexual persons away from Christ and his church.

11. That the General Assembly declare that these actions shall not be used to affect negatively the ordination rights of any deacon, elder or minister who has been ordained prior to this date in the Presbyterian Church in the United States.

Report Regarding the
Study of Homosexuality
Background

The issue of homosexuality and homosexual behavior was introduced to the 1972 PCUS General Assembly through a commissioner's resolution. (cf. 1972 GA *Minutes,* p. 182) This resolution was referred to the (then existent) Council on Church and Society for study, and subsequently became part of the agenda of its successor, the Council on Theology and Culture, by action of the 1973 General Assembly. (1973 GA *Minutes,* p. 113)

The 1974 and 1975 General Assemblies granted the Council on Theology and Culture extensions for this study, a fact called to the attention of the 1976 General Assembly by an overture from the Presbytery of Fayetteville. (1976 GA *Minutes,* p. 58–59) This overture was referred "as a matter of concern and information" to the Council on Theology and Culture with the following instructions:

> (a) That the 116th General Assembly express its sense of urgency concerning this matter with the request that this study become a priority item with the Council on Theology and Culture in anticipation if at all possible of a completed report to the 117th General Assembly.

> (b) That commissioners to the 116th General Assembly who wish to express their feelings, concerns and viewpoints in regard to this issue be encouraged to do so,

in writing, to the Council on Theology and Culture at their earliest opportunity: and that the Council on Theology and Culture be instructed to give full and serious attention to each expressed viewpoint in their deliberating and drafting of a completed report.

(c) That the Council on Theology and Culture be instructed by the 116th General Assembly to give thorough consideration to other denominational statements expressing their concerns and viewpoints on this issue, especially those statements of other members of our Reformed tradition such as the 188th General Assembly of the UPCUSA and the statement issued in 1970 by the Lutheran Church in America. (*Ibid.,* p. 215)

Study Paper

The Council on Theology and Culture presented to the 1977 General Assembly a study paper entitled "The Church and Homosexuality: A Preliminary Study" which was "endorsed as a basis of study" and authorized for distribution to the church along with a study guide. (1977 GA *Minutes,* pp. 318–346) "Presbyteries, sessions, individual churches and church members" were requested "to study the paper and respond with data and suggestions to the Council by May 1, 1978." The Council was instructed to appoint, direct and fund a task force "to receive the data and suggestions from the church, continue the study of homosexuality and make further recommendations to a subsequent General Assembly in the light of the responses received from the church."

Also the 1977 General Assembly adopted the following statements:

> That the 117th General Assembly express love and pastoral concern for homosexual persons and the need for the Church to stand for just treatment of homosexual persons in our society in regard to their civil liberties, equal rights, and protection under the law from social and economic discrimination which is due all citizens.
>
> Although we confess our need for more light and pray for spiritual guidance for the Church on this matter, we now believe that homosexuality falls short of God's plan for sexual relationships and urge the Church to seek the best ways for witnessing to God's moral standards and for ministering to homosexual persons concerning the love of God in Jesus Christ. (*Ibid.,* p. 174)

The paper sent to the church for study sought to aid those using it to grapple with various questions surrounding the topic of homosexuality in the present social situation. The distinction in definition of homosexual orientation and homosexual behavior was considered important in reviewing the causes and character of homosexuality. Ethical and theological presuppositions were noted and interpretations of biblical teachings about homosexuality were outlined in order to clarify alternatives before the church and the implications of each alternative for the church. Possible guidelines for making decisions about homosexuality and homosexual persons concluded the study document.

This study paper represented the Council's review of the available scientific information and biblical and theological considerations on the subject and described current patterns of thinking about the issue of homosexuality in the Christian community. Since it was designed to be a study paper to provide a basis for discussion, it did not recommend a specific position. The fact of its existence and availability through Materials Distribution Service, 341 Ponce de Leon Avenue, N.E. Atlanta, Georgia, 30308, make it unnecessary to cover the same ground in this report. In the judgment of the Council the study paper represents a useful review of the subject for discussion and study in the church.

Responses to the Study Paper

1. Who responded?

a. Eleven presbyteries in the Presbyterian Church in the United States overtured the 1978 General Assembly regarding the issue of homosexuality. (cf. 1978 GA *Minutes,* pp. 182, 190) Additionally ten other presbyteries sent reports of position statements or official responses of these presbyteries directly to the Council. These presbyteries are located in the following synods: Red River—1, Mid South— 7, Southeast—8, North Carolina—3, Florida—2. No responses were received from presbyteries in Mid-America and The Virginias.

b. Two-hundred twenty-five church sessions sent official responses. Two-hundred seventy-nine churches, including those which had study groups as well as session and diaconate studies, sent responses. This represents 7% of the churches of the denomination. However, the majority of the responding churches are of above average size, are representative of most regions of the church, and cover the rural, suburban, urban spectrum.

c. There were four-hundred eighty-five individual responses from session and diaconate members and eleven-hundred forty-seven responses from interested and concerned church members and others. The majority of those reporting indicated that they had used the study paper.

2. What did they say?

Several responses expressed appreciation for the opportunity to study the issue. About the same number were critical of the study, expressing amazement that the church would even consider such an issue. Along with those who suggested the continuance and expansion of the study there were as many who counselled termination of the project.

The convictions expressed in those communications can be characterized in the following summary:

a. The biblical teaching is that humankind is in a fallen, sinful state and homosexuality specifically is one manifestation of our sinful nature. It is a departure from God's intention, an abomination to God, a distortion of the order of creation and a threat to family life and social order. Several responses compared homosexuality with adultery, fornication, etc., quoting scripture and portions of Question 139 of the Larger Catechism. Several responses were critical of the study paper accusing it of attempting to explain away the clear teaching of scripture. A few individual responses expressed the view that homosexuality is a sickness (psychosexual disorder, sexual abnormality, retarded development). Only a few individual responses stated the conviction that it is a legitimate alternate life style or that it is a sin only when it hurts others. Quite a few muted a flat condemnation with a note of reserved caution. The distinction between homosexual orientation and homosexual activity/practice was given little attention except in those few responses from persons who were involved in some way with ministry to or counseling with homosexual persons. However, even in the most condemnatory statements the expression "homosexual practice or behavior" was prominent.

b. The responsibility of the church to show love, compassion, pastoral concern and to minister to and with persons struggling with homosexual tendencies was strongly affirmed by the vast majority of responses. The only specific provision of a church court for carrying out this ministry was made by one presbytery (Orange) which began a "fund for the rehabilitation of homosexuals within the bounds of this presbytery." The general assumption expressed was that ministry should be offered by individuals, with courts of original jurisdiction (presbyteries and sessions) dealing with appropriate situations. No suggestion was made for a program of ministry supported by the General Assembly.

There were some suggestions that homosexual behavior should be repented of and forsaken before the assumption of church membership. However, equal attention was given to the nature of church membership based on the vows stated in the *Book of Church Order* (210–5) which call for profession of faith in Christ (BCO-7–1). In this context one presbytery (Wilmington) endorsed the statement, "We believe that since the primary qualification for church membership is acceptance of Jesus Christ as Lord, one cannot refuse church membership to those who by accepting Christ are already members of his Body."

Regardless of how vehement and judgmental the responses claiming the sinfulness of homosexual practice there was this equally strong concern expressed for ministry with homosexual persons. Related to this concern is the question, "What does contact with homosexual persons do to one's perspective?" The responses indicate that it is felt that this depends upon the type of encounter. Several individual responses shared news stories of violence involving homosexual persons or personal stories of family tragedies. Other responses indicated that homosexual persons participated in the study process. Because of this involvement the individuals and study groups were more unclear, tentative and hesitant in their responses. As indicated in a comparison of such responses, where there is a greater distance from self-affirming homosexual persons, either in miles or attitudes, there tends to be more negative reactions to them.

c. The questions of whether or not avowed, practicing homosexual persons should be ordained by the church as Ministers of the Word, ruling elders or deacons was only an implicit aspect of the study paper. The question had not been raised in any official actions of the General Assembly of the Presbyterian Church in the United States. However, the question was made explicit through the presbytery overtures to the 1978 General Assembly. That Assembly made this question official material for consideration in the present report.

Several of the presbyteries either by sending overtures or by taking an official position have, by that very action, declared their stand against the ordination of avowed, practicing homosexuals. The majority of sessions and most individuals who responded to the study paper and expressed themselves on this issue, were opposed to such ordination. The reasons given for this opposition, besides referring to biblical statements of condemnation of the sinfulness of homosexual activity, were that the church cannot under any circumstances approve of homosexuality and to ordain avowed, practicing homosexuals, by precept and by example, would be improper and inappropriate.

Actions of the 1978 General Assembly

The 1978 General Assembly honored the process of study and response adopted by the 1977 General Assembly by the following action:

1. That the many overtures concerning what the church's position should be regarding homosexuality and related matters, such as the ordination of self-affirmed and practicing homosexuals, pastoral care of homosexuals and

their families, church membership of self-affirmed homosexuals, etc., be answered by adopting the following:

a. That the General Assembly refer the Overtures to the Council on Theology and Culture, to assist that Council in its continuing preparation of its report and recommendations for the 119th General Assembly.

b. That the General Assembly reaffirm the statements adopted by the 117th General Assembly.

c. That the General Assembly commend to the Council on Theology and Culture as additional resource material the 1978 study papers of the United Presbyterian Church in the U.S.A. and the Policy Statement and Recommendations adopted by the 190th General Assembly of that church.

d. That the General Assembly note that the Committee recommends the above on the basis of its awareness.

    1. That the study of homosexuality is of great complexity;

    2. That the 117th General Assembly directed the Council on Theology and Culture to prepare a comprehensive study based on the conscientious responses from the membership and courts of the Church;

    3. That many Church courts and individuals have complied with the 117th General Assembly's request that responses to the preliminary study be sent directly to the Council on Theology and Culture;

    4. That the Church can be strengthened by the participation of its members in the study and debate of this issue, especially when the participation reflects Christ-like compassion and love towards homosexually-oriented individuals and towards those of differing convictions;

    5. That the Church's comprehensive study of homosexuality with recommendations will be presented to the 119th General Assembly.

e. That the General Assembly further note that the Committee wishes to express its appreciation to those Church courts which communicated their concerns about the homosexuality issue by overturing this General Assembly and to assure them that their concerns were heard by this Assembly and will be considered in the drafting of the report for 1979.

STUDY GUIDE TO DEFINITIVE GUIDANCE

Jack L. Stotts

For the Leader

- Each student should have a copy of this book or have access to one. Also, each member should bring a Bible to every class.

- Each class session should be opened and closed with prayer.

- The teacher is to be well informed about the topic but is not understood to be the person most knowledgeable about the subject in general or any of its particular points. He or she is primarily to facilitate class discussion and to clarify issues.

- The teacher, in consultation with the class, may invite knowledgeable resource persons to address the class about a particular area of the subject. If so, the teacher should make clear to the resource person(s) the need to leave ample time for discussion.

- The teacher should, in consultation with the person or persons responsible for Christian education in the church, determine the number and times of class meetings.

- This study guide assumes that classes will be small enough to enable and encourage discussion. If the class is large (say, over twenty), the teacher should consider modifying the suggested approach. For example, one could have a lecture/discussion format, with discussion in small groups following a presentation. Whatever methodology is chosen, interaction among participants in the class should be a priority.

- Set a time for evaluation near the midpoint in the schedule of classes. Such an evaluation could lead to a change in the topics to be addressed, the length of time allotted for the class, or other alterations that would enhance the study's effectiveness.

- The organization of the class by topics, as indicated below, is understood to be flexible—able to be extended or compressed to meet the class's needs.

- An assumption is that class participants will read and reflect in advance on the assignments and will bring their comments and questions to the next meeting. The teacher may choose each week to ask one or more members to initiate discussion the following week. The teacher's responsibilities are partially indicated above. Others include requesting appropriate resources for the class, for example, newsprint, tape, and markers. More substantively, the teacher shall help to establish a non-threatening and open atmosphere in the class, sensitive to the differing experiences and beliefs about the topic of homosexuality.

- The following guide should be understood as only one possibility of ordering the study of the issue of homosexuality.

Session 1
Introduction

Following prayer, the teacher should welcome the class members, inviting each one to introduce himself or herself, including saying what brings them to this particular class.

The teacher will discuss the context of the study, pointing out that its sources lie in the emerged and emerging public attention to issues of homosexuality and the church's sense of need to respond. Call to the class's attention that the initiative for the denomination's consideration of the topic of homosexuality goes back to the 112th General Assembly (1972) of the Presbyterian Church in the United States (PCUS), where a commissioner resolution regarding homosexuality was referred to the Council on Church and Society, which subsequently forwarded the resolution to that denomination's Council on Theology and Culture. That Council brought to the 116th General Assembly of the PCUS (1977) the study paper "The Church and Homosexuality: A Preliminary Study," which is included in this book. That also led to the position paper "Homosexuality and the Church," which was presented to the 118th General Assembly of the PCUS (1979) and is presented in this book.

In the United Presbyterian Church in the United States of America (UPCUSA), the Presbyteries of New York and the Palisades overtured the General Assembly for guidance on the question of the ordination of "avowed practicing homosexuals." That overture brought the document "The Church and Homosexuality" to the 1978 General Assembly of the UPCUSA, the policy statement and recommendations of which are in this book.

Expectations

This class will focus on homosexuality in its various facets, not on the issue of the ordination of gays and lesbians, or bisexual and transgendered persons. The ordination question will be addressed, but it should not monopolize the class's attention.

The teacher should make clear that this class is not designed to be a forum of advocacy but a forum for understanding: understanding homosexuality, understanding the church's attitude and behavior toward homosexuals, and understanding ourselves no matter what our sexual orientation. The teacher could speak of the class as a neutral zone, where one can openly discuss personal attitudes and beliefs with the understanding that what is said will be treated with respect and openness. The class will welcome diverse perspectives. It will also seek to offer a safe haven for the participants. The teacher may wish to emphasize the fact that the matter of homosexuality is one that has been and remains highly volatile, filled with emotions and with judgments that may have evolved and are still evolving through the power of the Spirit of the transforming God whom we have known through Jesus Christ.

Having gone through the expectations as to how the class is to function, the teacher should direct the students to the foreword to this book by Stated Clerk Clifton Kirkpatrick. The teacher may wish to go over the foreword and point out salient information and points included in it.

Finally, conclude the session by having the students identify questions and concerns they have and that they would hope to have included in the class discussion. Ask a class member to put those items on newsprint or a chalkboard to be used for future reference.

The teacher should ask the class to read the entire 1977 document prior to its next meeting, giving special attention to Sections I and II, "The Definition of Homosexuality" and "The Causes and Character of Homosexuality."

Ask a class member to prepare to summarize this session at the start of the next meeting.

Close with prayer.

Session 2

Definition and the Causes and Character of Homosexuality

The class should be opened with prayer.

Following prayer, the person designated to do so will summarize the last meeting of the class.

Ask each member of the class to identify questions and concerns that have arisen from their readings. Those who prefer not to respond to the request, or who have not read the assignments, may "pass" or express their issues about defining homosexuality and its causes and character.

Have a member of the class put the responses on newsprint or a chalkboard. Ask if any other matters have been overlooked. Identify points of agreement and disagreement.

Next, put this definition of homosexuality from the book on the board or newsprint: "In popular usage the word is restricted to explicitly sexual attraction and/or activity between members of the same sex." Ask if there is agreement about that definition and, if not, what corrections would be suggested. The goal is to come to a consensus about this important starting point in the study. If that does not occur, proceed with the discussion, recognizing diversity around this matter of definition.

Move to the specific issue of distinguishing homosexual condition or orientation and activity. Try to assure that these differing categories are understood. Point out the importance of that distinction in the following chapters in all the papers in the book. Go back to the initial listing of issues and concerns identified at the beginning of the class and see if each can be placed under one or both of these categories.

This 1977 document explicitly adopts a continuum of homosexuality. Have that continuum before the class in handout form and read it with the group. Point out that the continuum derives from an early study called the Kinsey Report, published in 1948. This report is now dated but still useful. Do class members agree with the continuum? If yes, why? If not, why? Are there helpful things about it for looking at homosexuality?

Move on to the section titled Causes and Character of Homosexuality (page 8). Identify the issues raised in this section of the essay. Have the class list the issues that are in the section. Emphasize that disagreement exists about causality. Decisions about this issue will influence future outcomes. The call in the document for those dealing with homosexuality is to modesty about conclusions.

Make assignments for next week, including reading section III of the 1977 report (page 9).

Ask for a volunteer to begin the next class with a summary of what was done in the current class.

Close with prayer.

Session 3

Some Fundamental Ethical and Theological Presuppositions

Begin with prayer, then ask for the summary of the last session.

Identify and discuss the four presuppositions in Section III of the 1977 paper:

1. The individuality of homosexual persons

2. The Church's involvement

3. The relation between homosexual orientation and homosexual activity

4. The possibility of change

You may want to have members of the class selected in advance to lead the class in understanding each proposition. Identify positive and negative judgments that pertain to the topic of each presupposition. Identify disagreements that arise out of a consideration of each.

Call to the attention of the participants the basic issue that surfaces again, namely, the distinction between orientation and activity. You may want to involve an outside resource person or persons to speak to the change question. Identify the important distinction between indeterminism and determinism.

Summarize the discussion. Have participants read section IV (pages 12–22) for the next meeting.

Close with prayer.

Session 4

Interpretations of Biblical Teaching about Homosexuality

Begin with prayer. Have a participant summarize the last class, or do so yourself.

Underscore that the issue under discussion in this session is biblical interpretation. Someone has said that the fundamental distinction among those for whom the Bible is a source of authority is between those who acknowledge that they interpret the Scripture and those who say they don't.

You may want to suggest a simple formula for interpretation. One useful approach is to first inquire, "What does the passage say? What did it mean to the people of the day?" Then ask, "What does it mean to me or to us?" Using that or some other device, break up into smaller groups of three or four to explore certain biblical passages that are relevant to considering homosexuality. They include the passages mentioned in this section from Genesis, Leviticus, Romans, 1 Corinthians, and Timothy. If the class is relatively small, one might break into two groups, one to consider the Old Testament and one the New Testament passages.

After about twenty minutes, ask each group to share their findings with each other, with any conclusions they might make about a biblical understanding of homosexuality.

Next, assign for next week the rereading of the "Total Biblical Witness" section of the paper (pages 19–23). Ask for volunteers, each one to present one of the two arguments in the section sympathetically and with a degree of advocacy for each. These presentations are to elicit discussion for the whole class.

Designate someone to begin the next meeting of the class by summarizing this week's discussion.

Close with prayer.

Session 5

Total Biblical Witness

Begin with prayer, and then a summary of the previous session.

Open by reading or writing on a chalkboard or newsprint this crucial sentence: "The fundamental question is whether or not God's creative and redemptive purposes for human sexuality relates exclusively to male-female relatedness" (pages 19–22). Can the traditional understanding of authentic and legitimate sexual relationships for heterosexual Christians be extended to include some homosexual practices?

Ask in advance two members of the class to be prepared to speak on the two arguments presented in the text of this section. One is supportive of the traditional interpretation that "recognizes only male-female relatedness as the proper expression of human sexuality." The other contends that God's intended relationships of human sexuality can be legitimately expressed in homosexual relationships. They should summarize the points made and the positions put forth, including points of convergence and of divergence.

The teacher should identify that a basic issue in this section is the ongoing discussions of the authority of Scripture.

The teacher may ask for three volunteers to present for the following session the three options and their consequences for the church that conclude the 1977 paper.

The assignment for the next week is to read the sections on Alternatives Before the Church and Guidelines (pages 23–30).

Close with prayer.

Session 6

Alternatives before the Church and Guidelines

Begin with prayer, then have someone summarize the last class, or do so yourself.

Begin this session by having two presenters, one to lead the discussion on alternatives, one on guidelines. Follow with group discussion. In a sense, the section on alternatives is the central practical issue. Ask each person to place himself or herself as the leader, lay or clergy, within a congregation. Ask, "What position would you generally support? Why? What would be the specific consequences of support of one approach?"

The class should next turn its attention to specific guidelines, going over each one in the whole group. This session of the class should close with people summarizing what they have learned and how they may have thus far received new insights and if they have experienced change of heart or mind as a result of the course.

Next week's assignment should be to read all of the material in the documents from actions of the 190th General Assembly of the UPCUSA (1978) and the position paper adopted by the General Assembly of the PCUS (1979), which made for the most part minor changes in wording and added one paragraph on the topic of sin as a condition of the fall.

The class should be reminded that they have gone beyond the halfway point of the class and will spend a few minutes during the next class session evaluating the course thus far and making adjustments for the rest of the allotted time.
Close with prayer.

Session 7

Response to a Request for Guidance, Part 1

Open with prayer.

Present a summary of the last session.

Point out the nature of the position paper and the social policy statement. By action of each General Assembly, the 1978 and 1979 documents have official standing in the denominations and thus consequences for the church's life and ministry. The text of the material in these statements provides grounds for conclusions and recommendations that are an integral part of each paper.

These policies affirmed by both churches on human sexuality were carried over into the reunited churches that came together in 1983. They include the adoption of the policy on homosexual ordination and recommendations. A great deal of often contentious debate and disagreement has occurred and continues today about the "definitive guidance" decision. The arguments are around the issues of ordination and the biblical and theological interpretations related to the ordination of homosexual persons.

Point out that both the 1978 and 1979 papers are packed with material that is complex and charged with meaning. In its original form, the 1978 report was accompanied by an extended essay that the General Assembly accepted

---

as an aid to study. That complete document is available at the Presbyterian Church (U.S.A.) Web site, http://www.pcusa.org/oga/publications/church-and-homosexuality.pdf.

Note that the class will have three sessions on the 1978 and 1979 statements. As the two documents are so alike, assignments may be made on only one; the 1979 position paper is the better one to use because it includes one critical addition and deletes nothing of primary significance from the 1978 policy statement. The current class will focus on the sections "Homosexuality Within a Theological Context" and "Scripture and Homosexuality." The next class session will deal with the other sections of the papers. The concluding session for the class will explore the definitive guidance policy and the recommendations of both documents.

Begin by noting the similarities and differences in these documents and the 1977 study. For example, all begin with Jesus Christ as the agent of God's creating and redeeming grace. Here one could discuss the meaning of repentance and the power of God's Spirit to bring about change.

All these documents give a high place to scientific sources as necessary for understanding the causes of homosexuality. Both conclude that these causes are remarkably numerous and diverse. These extrabiblical sources have an enormous impact when it comes to making judgments about causality. On the other hand, they are not determinative of theological and biblical convictions. Discuss the difference between "determinacy" and "indeterminacy." The position paper elicits the ongoing discussion between nature and nurture. Also, the paper recognizes the dynamic nature of human sexuality and leaves the question of cause theoretically open to new scientific understandings.

A basic difference between the 1977 and 1979 documents and the earlier study on homosexuality is the approach to the nature of sin. Both affirm that homosexuality is a condition. A new element is present in the 1979 position paper: the affirmation that sin is not to be identified initially at least with behaviors but is rather a manifestation of the fallen world. We all are residents of a fallen world, a world of broken humankind, of which homosexuality is an expression, though in no way the exclusive one. Discuss what it means when one says that homosexuality as a condition is the result of the fall. Have the class distinguish between sin and sins, sin as a condition of our being and sins as behaviors that manifest themselves in deeds contrary to God's will.

Point out that the weight of the argument from the sciences leans heavily toward the presupposition of indeterminacy, calling for repentance, which translated means voluntarily changing both one's "condition" and one's behavior. Ask the class to discuss their judgment about this.

Have the class identify other similarities and differences between the papers, as well as other issues.

With reference to the "Scripture and Homosexuality" section, have the class respond to any difference of approach to reading the Scripture that the class has considered previously. Look at the section on Genesis. Why is the statement on creation so important?

For the next session, ask the class to reread the 1979 statements on Church Membership, Ordination, Diversity and Unity in the Church, Ministry and Mission, and Decriminalization and Civil Rights. Have them bring to the class their questions and comments.

Close with prayer.

Session 8

Response to a Request for Guidance, Part 2

Open with prayer and a summary of the last session.

Begin by listing the topics to be covered in this session: Church Membership, Ordination, Pluralism and Unity in the Church, Ministry and Mission, Decriminalization and Civil Rights, Conclusion, and Recommendations.

Remind the class that ordination of homosexual persons remains a point of contention in the church today, twenty-five years after this study was done. Explore with the class the meaning of ordination. Have the class define its characteristics. Inquire into how ordination is viewed by members of the class. How does ordination differ from and build on the meaning of membership?

Under the category of diversity and unity in the church, you might want to invite the pastor or a leader whom he or she would select to speak to the class about the ongoing debate in the church on the ordination of homosexual persons. Questions to be discussed include:

- What is the current situation in the denomination with reference to ordination of overtly practicing homosexual persons?

- What boundaries, if any, are there to diversity and the commitments to unity?

- What characteristics are there of the ministry and mission of the church to and with homosexual persons?

- How do they differ from other forms of ministry and mission?

Ask the class to discuss court decisions and legislation passed since the 1978 and 1979 papers were adopted that moved to decriminalize private behavior between consenting adults. Also, ask what the class believes about different legislative initiatives that have sought to make it either legal or illegal for a union between two persons of the same sex to be recognized as a "marriage." What does the class think about "holy unions" as a civil or an ecclesiastical "right"?

Ask for someone to lead off the next session by summarizing the discussion during this session.

Assign as reading the guidance and recommendations adopted by the General Assemblies of both denominations in the 1978 and 1979 papers.

Close with prayer.

Session 9

Definitive Guidance
and Recommendations

Following prayer, have the person assigned to do so summarize the last session.

Move to considering definitive guidance. What does the class think about the appropriateness or inappropriateness of this direction? If the vote on adopting the definitive guidance policy were to be held today, what would be each person's vote? Divide the class into groups of three to five and ask them to discuss and vote on the policy. Ask the group to report their position(s) and give reasons for its vote. If there is not unanimity, give reasons for holding a different view than that of the majority.

Go through the recommendations and ask for comment on each. Ask if there are recommendations one would add today.

Ask the class members to be prepared for the next (and final) session to review the resources used in the class and to share their learnings and perspectives. Also, have them come prepared to identify issues or concerns that should be addressed more adequately or fully than they were.

Close with prayer.

Session 10
Review and Evaluation

Following prayer, review the original goals of the class: understanding homosexuality more adequately, understanding the church's stand on the subject, and understanding ourselves, no matter what our sexual orientation.

Encourage the class to share the understandings that have come from participation in the class. Identify issues of agreement and disagreement that remain in the church over the consideration of homosexuality, and specifically the ordination of avowed, practicing homosexuals.

Discuss the various stands that are being taken in the Presbyterian Church (U.S.A.), including compliance, whether in agreement or not; public rejection of the operative interpretation of "definitive guidance"; judicial charges brought against those who have not accepted the policy; and the policy toward those who continue their previous positions with reference to the judgment as to the criteria for ordination.

In conclusion, point out some of the common themes and issues that flow through the documents. A few are:

- The unanimous commitment to care for and welcome into membership homosexual persons, along with the confession and rejection of homophobia in the church and in the society.

- The affirmation of the authority of Scripture in shaping decisions about all ethical and theological issues.

- The centrality of Jesus Christ for the church's interpretation of and position on all matters of discipleship.

- The importance for churches to provide locations where consideration of such matters as homosexuality can be openly discussed in a way that reflects mutuality and openness.

- The significance of contemporary scientific views about the sources/causes of sexual orientation and behavior.

- The acknowledgment of unity and diversity and the search for a proper relationship between them as a context for life today in the church and in the society.

Ask for any closing concerns or needs, or any next steps that the class would like to see taken as a result of this study.

Close with a prayer to be offered together. Make copies of the prayer you use so all can join in praying. One example of such a prayer is:

> Gracious God, for the many gifts you shower upon us we are grateful indeed. We are grateful for the love of Jesus Christ which binds us together; we are grateful for the church, Christ's body, and rejoice in being members, speaking the truth as we understand it in love; and we are grateful for your Spirit which moves among us, granting us new and fresh understandings of the One who enables us to grow in faith, hope, and love.
>
> From the depths of our gratitude we ask for continued growth in knowledge and wisdom as we seek the way of the One who is the way, the truth, and the life, the One who by the Spirit gives us courage ". . . to hear the voices of peoples long silenced, and to work with others for justice, freedom and peace," striving "to serve Christ in our daily tasks."
>
> Through Jesus Christ we pray. Amen.